Walking Down the Manny Road: Inside Bolton's Football Hooligan Gangs

Doug Mitchell
(with Simon Eddisbury)

Fort Publishing Ltd

First published in 2011 by Fort Publishing Ltd, Old Belmont House,
12 Robsland Avenue, Ayr, KA7 2RW

© Doug Mitchell 2011

All rights reserved. No part of this publication may be reproduced, stored in a retrieval system, or transmitted, in any form or by any means, electronic, mechanical, photocopying, recording or otherwise, without the prior permission of the publishers and copyright holders.

Doug Mitchell has asserted his rights under the Copyright, Designs and Patents Act, 1988 to be recognised as the author of this work.

Printed by Bell and Bain Ltd, Glasgow

Typeset by 3btype.com

Graphic design by Mark Blackadder

Front-cover photograph by Kevan Jackson

ISBN: 978-1-905769-24-7

This book is dedicated to everyone who has stood his ground as a Bolton lad.

CONTENTS

It Was Written . . .		7
The Firms		9
Introduction		13
1	The Early Years	15
2	From the Streets to the Terraces	21
3	Punks and Skins	24
4	Boys, Dressers and Casuals	31
5	The Scum	36
6	The Scousers	49
7	The EDL Connection	55
8	The Youth	72
9	The Walkden Whites	87
10	Foreign Shores	95
11	Bristol City	114
12	The Baggies	120
13	Middlesbrough	124
14	Portsmouth	129
15	Blackpool	132
16	Blackburn	139
17	Preston	150
18	'We're All Off to Find the Cockneys'	156
19	Birmingham City Zulus	160
20	Ipswich	163
21	To Hull and Back	165
22	Hibs	168
23	Stoke	173
24	Doncaster	176
25	Oldham	180
26	Millwall	184

27	The Jacks	188
28	Wigan	192
29	Burnley	201
30	Lest We Forget . . .	204
31	Bolton versus Bolton	211
32	Operation Gamma	214
33	The Future	219

The Lingo   223

IT WAS WRITTEN . . .

Before I introduce myself, let's have a quick recap on what they've been saying about us over the years. It's important for you to see what other people have written about us before we describe ourselves to you in our own words, just so that you know what kind of things to expect in this book. If you're offended by shoplifting, graphic violence, heavy drinking and drug taking then this frank account of our lives is almost certainly not for you. On the other hand if you've always been intrigued by the darker side of football, read on and gain an insight into one of the country's most active hooligan firms. Opinions of our exploits are seldom favourable. The press hate us, the coppers hate us and even some of our own fans don't like us. Well I guess you can't please everyone!

'A notorious group of soccer thugs'
The Bolton News, 20 March 2000

'What kind of animals behave like this? It is an absolute disgrace!'
Bolton resident Sue Littleton, quoted in the *Bolton Evening News*, 22 February 2003

'They are violent people whose sole aim was to cause as much disruption as they could throughout the country'
Chief Superintendent Frank Halligan, key figure in Operation Gamma, which was a crackdown on Bolton hooligans

'They are worse than the notorious Birmingham, Leeds and Chelsea fans'
A spokesman for the Barnsley police force, quoted in the *Bolton Evening News*

'One of the most notorious sets of hooligans'
White Love fanzine, 4 April 1988

'Thugs who peddle terror in the name of Bolton Wanderers'
Bolton Evening News, 19 May 1990

'The consequences of their thuggish actions are very serious'
Chief Superintendent Roberts, Greater Manchester Police

'Well-organised gangs of louts, which included some of Britain's worst football thugs'
Bolton Evening News, 4 May 1990

'Some of the most violent football hooligans in Britain'
Daily Mail, October 2009

'Yobs in £10,000 contract to get Cantona'
Daily Mirror, 1997

'You are a disgrace to mankind'
The judge at the end of the Operation Gamma trial at Liverpool Crown Court

THE FIRMS

Here is a brief introduction to the smaller mobs that are collectively known as the Cuckoo Boys:

The Tonge Moor Stanley Boys

There has always been a strong hooligan contingent on the Tonge Moor estate, although they were originally just known as 'Tonge Moor'. The 'Stanley Boys' part came about after a spate of knife attacks carried out in the mid 1980s. They are our most notorious firm, known for taking blades to the matches. You can criticise them all you want but they didn't invent the phenomenon of carrying tools. The Scousers and the Mancs were doing it well before them. If you are involved in football violence there is always a chance that you're going to get stabbed, slashed, bricked or bottled. It is part of being a hooligan, something that is never going to change.

The Horwich Casuals

They were Bolton's first casual mob. They were always the best-dressed firm, probably because a few of them had money. You couldn't let their sharp dress sense fool you though. They were game lads and they liked their weapons. A few of them got picked up for firearms offences during a riot in Bury a couple of years back, proving there are worse things than knives that you can bring to a row.

Farnworth

We weren't always accepted by the other lads because Farnworth is a separate town and they didn't see it as part of Bolton. Still, a fair few people have come here looking for a fight and they've learned the hard way not to take the piss. If you come down here mob-handed then you'll have a row on your hands. There used to be stabbings every week and it's not the type of place in which you can throw your weight around and expect to get away with it.

Great Lever

They were known for thieving from shops and service stations on the way to games. They had a mob of around eighty lads and the boys from Daubhill would go with them to the matches to bulk their numbers out.

Little Lever

Close allies of the Farnworth mob and the Tonge Moor Stanley Boys. They used to drink with us in Farnworth on a Friday night and had some sound lads with them.

West Houghton

A smallish firm but as game as fuck.

Morris Dangers

They're from an area called Morris Green in Great Lever and their name is a reference to the local non-league team, the Morris Dancers.

Billy Whiz Fan Club

This is a group from Halliwell, whose name was chosen because it had the same initials as Bolton Wanderers Football Club. It was also a reference to their love of amphetamines, although they didn't take any more or less drugs than the other mobs around at the time. Speed was rife during that period and all of Bolton's main firms liked to have a dabble every now and again.

Astley Bridge Mob

They've got forty handy lads with them but they have fallen out with a lot of the other firms in recent years.

Breightmet

A bunch of lads from another rough part of the town, next to Tonge Moor.

Halliwell Cutters Crew

Halliwell is one of the toughest places in Bolton so it is little wonder there is such a game bunch of lads living there. I've got some good mates in their firm and they can definitely look after themselves.

Blackrod

A small firm from a small village but they have always had some game lads with them.

Newbury Cavemen

I would say that 95 per cent of them are off their fucking heads. They are always robbing shops and service stations and they even tried to rob a park bench at one game I went to with them.

Bolton Youth

The Youth are even wilder than we were back when we first came on the scene. They aren't scared of anything and they are always networking with other firms. One of their mob could bang into another football lad while he was out with his missus and he would be straight on his case, trying to get his number to arrange a row.

As you can see, virtually every area of Bolton and Farnworth has had its own firm at one time or another. There is a definite gang culture round here and all of the different estates were rowing with one another long before football entered the equation. The Wanderers were a unifying factor. They brought the smaller street gangs together to fight against rival towns and cities. Areas that were once kicking the shit out of each other suddenly began to work together . . . and a mighty alliance was formed.

INTRODUCTION

The reason that I'm doing this book is to put the record straight on a couple of issues. Firstly, I want to let the public know the truth behind the things they have read about in other hooligan books. If you believe what those who have come before me have written you will no doubt conclude that we are all superhuman and that none of us ever ran away from a fight. However, in reality, every firm has been on its toes at one time or another and we've all been done as well. It doesn't make you any less of a man; it just means that you are less of a bullshitter, simply because you have had the balls to admit that you're not invincible.

Secondly, I want to try and dispel the image of the hooligan as a brain-dead thug who goes around robbing old grannies and laying into innocent football fans. The only people that we bring trouble to are those who go looking for it. Okay so there may have been the odd person who was in the wrong place at the wrong time and ended up getting a couple of digs by mistake but it's a rare occurrence. We have never intended to cause harm to anyone who wasn't up for a fight.

The other major failing of the average hooligan book is the author's insistence on portraying himself as the firm's main player. I am not a top boy and I have never claimed to be one. Bolton has had a number of top boys throughout the years and they have hailed from different parts of the town. Nowadays nobody is the top lad although there are a couple of people who pull the strings and who can get a mob together. Saying that, I have been involved in football violence for over three decades and I have seen a thing or two in my time. I have been there since the Cuckoo Boys were in their infancy and they have stuck with me through thick and thin, which is the reason I have decided to make this a book about the firm as a whole rather than using it as a personal ego trip. In the interests of representing the views of the entire mob, I have enlisted the help of seven other Bolton lads, who will be contributing whenever they feel that they have something worth saying. They are:

Kevin
The leader of the Bolton Youth firm.

Phil
Phil has been involved with the Cuckoo Boys since the age of sixteen and he is now thirty-six. He was mainly active during the 1990s and he has been in his fair share of scrapes throughout the years. Nowadays he takes his kids to the games so he is no longer a hooligan, although he maintains that once you've had your first taste of football violence, you can never truly call it quits.

Graham
One of Bolton's top younger lads, I met him at a game against Lokomotiv Plovdiv in Bulgaria.

Chris
Another member of our youth mob.

S
A lad from Little Lever who has been retired from the scene for some time now.

P
A lad from a village called Darcy Lever, between Bolton and Little Lever.

Great Lever Lad
He was active during the Eighties and hasn't been involved for twenty years.

1
THE EARLY YEARS

My story begins back in the quiet suburban enclave of Gracemouth in Edinburgh. It was the type of place where the local community got on well with one another and I grew up in a loving and stable family. We weren't massively well off but we weren't particularly poor either.

When I was eight years old, my father broke the news to me that we were moving to a small, former industrial town just outside of Bolton. There weren't many jobs going in Scotland at the time and my granddad, grandma, Auntie Anne and Uncle Tommy had already moved to Farnworth in search of higher-paid work. It was an opportunity for us to better ourselves. I was sad that I had to leave my old friends behind and start afresh but it was a small price to pay for the wealth of benefits the move would bring about.

'You'll make a new set of mates in no time at all,' my dad assured me. 'I'm sure there will be plenty of other kids your age there.'

In Farnworth we lived with my nan at first and my aunty lived on the same street. After we'd settled into our new surroundings, we moved into a house on Rawson Street, where my dad still lives today. There were loads of other families living nearby and I soon got to know the children in the surrounding estates. We would while away the hours playing football on Farnworth Park and wandering around in the local woodland, making rope swings and playing at being explorers. If we ever had a disagreement, we would be friends again the next day. Or, if it was football-related, one of the kids would storm off home with the ball. It was a happy, carefree part of my youth, although I was about to find out about the underlying gang culture. My secondary school, George Tomlinson's, was a lot different to my junior school, St Peter's. At Tomlinson's we had a bitter rivalry with St James's and Harper Green and we were expected to take part in organised fights to defend the honour of our school.

Most of the kids from our rival schools hailed from either Newbury or Highfield, two of Farnworth's roughest estates. The lads from our school would team up with the pupils from the local Catholic school, St Gregg's, and we'd have mass brawls in order to find out which school was the hardest. It was the first time I'd been involved in recreational violence and I took to it straight away. The boys who were the most willing to fight would get the highest levels of respect. It was a way of showing off to the other kids on the estate.

Eventually, fighting with rival schools progressed into fighting with rival areas. We fought with Newbury, Highfield and Green Lane in Bolton and it soon got to the stage where we had to be very careful about where we went. Farnworth and Bolton were both very clannish in those days and you could easily get a kicking for being in the wrong place at the wrong time.

The Highfield Boot Boys were our worst enemies. Highfield is only about two miles away from Newbury and they were always teaming up with the Newbury Cavemen, who controlled those parts. With gangs from two of Farnworth's roughest estates gunning for us, we rarely had to venture outside of our own area, as they were always trekking into central Farnworth, looking to do us in.

When we weren't fighting it out with our rivals, we were getting up to all kinds of other mischief. There was a big, fat, epileptic guy who owned a shop in the town centre and we would go down there and rob the pinball machines while he was having his fits. It was a cruel thing to do but you don't really think about the consequences of your actions when you're that age. If I saw him nowadays I would offer to buy him a pint to make up for it but I guess you develop more of a conscience as you get older.

As the years went by, all the main gangs in Farnworth gradually merged. We kept bumping into lads from Highfield and Newbury down at the local pub and ended up being good mates with a few of them.

The animosity between the different estates slowly eroded until there was no-one left to row with. We soon realised that we were going to have to find ourselves a new set of rivals. As luck would have it, a gang from the neighbouring village of Little Hulton had arrived on the scene, looking to show us what they were made of.

Little Hulton is basically a little piece of Salford that has been transplanted into the gap between Farnworth and Manchester. It is a giant overspill estate, which was used to rehouse all of the old residents from the Coronation Street-style terraced houses that were demolished in the late 1950s. We nicknamed their firm the Spillamies because they had spilled over from Salford and we waged war on them at every available opportunity.

Now that the three main Farnworth firms were allies, we were pulling mobs of up to one-hundred-and-fifty lads. It was no longer just fist fighting either. Knives, sticks and bottles were all used on a regular basis. The levels of violence gradually intensified and we became more than just a group of troublesome school kids. In the process we made a name for ourselves throughout the neighbouring towns and villages.

Most of our rows with the Spillamies took place either on the motorway bridge over the M61 or on the set of fields that separated Farnworth from Little Hulton. We have had some epic battles with them over the years. I remember a brawl in which one of their lads got stabbed and another was thrown over the side of the bridge into the path of the oncoming traffic. The streets were like a war zone that day. There were hundreds of us and hundreds of them and the coppers were setting their dogs on us and chasing us through the estates, sirens blaring. I loved every single minute of it.

When we got a little older, our battles with the Spillamies continued in a place called Blighty's in Farnworth town centre. It was a massive club with two different levels and a big balcony overlooking the dance floor. It was popular with hen nights and stag parties and people travelled from all over the north of England to attend the cabaret nights. As with any venue of its size, Blighty's has encountered its fair share of trouble over the years. The local street gangs from Highfield, Newbury, Central Farnworth and Moses Gate would go there every Friday and Saturday night and end up brawling with the out-of-towners. Outsiders seemed to think they could come to Farnworth and throw their weight around without us kicking off. The Scousers were the worst. I remember when one of them threw a beer glass off the balcony and it hit a local girl in the face. She was cut up pretty badly and, within a matter of minutes, we were all over the cunts, kicking and punching them for all we were worth. We beat the fuck out of the dirty Scouse bastards and then we twatted them again outside. The bouncers were also weighing into them and, if I remember correctly, a group of coppers eventually joined in and gave them a couple of digs for injuring the girl.

That was Farnworth for you. If you came looking for a fight you wouldn't have long to wait.

The day after our run-in with the Scousers, I found out that a good friend of mine had stabbed one of them during the mêlée. I won't give his name because he does a lot for the local community nowadays but he was a decent lad and I remember thinking, 'It's not enough, you should have carved up the lot of them.' He ended up getting sent down but, if you ask me, they should have given him a medal. You can't go throwing glasses about and expect to get away with it. At the end of the day, that Scouse bastard got what was coming to him. It was his own fault for ruining that poor girl's night.

The Mancs were the other main group that we had trouble with. For some unknown reason, a lot of people can't tell the difference between Boltonians and Mancunians, although it is blindingly obvious to anybody with a bit of common sense. The difference is that they're the fucking scum of the earth and we're not. Some of the other Cuckoo Boys have such a deep-seated loathing for anything vaguely associated with Manchester that they often tell me they wish they had been alive to see the Munich air disaster. Although I am in no way condoning that sentiment, their words are testament to the levels of hatred that exist between the honest, hardworking people of Bolton and the dirty Red twats that live a few miles to the south-east of us.

Our intense rivalry with the Mancs was fuelled by the way they would invade our nightclubs every Friday night, swaggering around as if they owned the place. So-called hard men from Wythenshawe would travel into Bolton looking for a fight and we would give them a kick up the arse and send them on their way.

Wythenshawe is Manchester's biggest council estate and its residents seem to think that they can do whatever the hell they want. Well not in fucking Bolton they can't! Every time they showed their faces we would beat them black and blue and send them straight back to where they had come from. The Mancs eventually decided that enough was enough and a huge horde of them turned up at a local pub, looking to do us in.

Within a matter of minutes, all the punters from the surrounding boozers had descended on the pub, looking to do the Wythenshawe mob some serious damage. Most of them managed to get away but one of their lads got left behind and he was taught a lesson he will never forget. He was kicked to fuck and a metal newsstand was slammed into his face, leaving an ugly lump of blood and gristle where his head had once been. He spent the next few weeks in hospital and let's just say he won't be posing for pictures any time soon.

The local paper reported that the attack was carried out by a 'notorious gang from Bolton known as the Cuckoo Boys'. At that stage, the firm didn't really have a name so I don't know where they got that one from. Someone must have been feeding them dodgy information. Just as we were beginning to think that our fifteen minutes of fame were over, I picked up the morning papers and came across a second factually incorrect article. We had made the headlines yet again, only this time we were known as the 'Mongoose Cuckoo Boys'. It was eventually shortened back down to 'Cuckoo Boys' and it's a title that has stuck with us ever since.

So there you have it, the name of one of the country's most active hooligan firms was originally based upon a mistake by the local press. What had started off as a collection of area-based gangs adopted a moniker devised by the media and gradually came together to form a single, unified mob. Wythenshawe's inability to turn us over was a clear indication of what we were capable of, although the best was yet to come, as the gamest lads from every area of Bolton were about to band together to fight for their local team. It was time for us to harness our territorialism and direct it against a set of common enemies.

After all, we had stood our ground against a firm from one of the biggest estates in the country and emerged victorious.

Over the years, our priorities shifted from fighting with the Mancs to fighting with rival sets of supporters. Football channelled my aggression into something specific. There is no point in having a row if you are not going to achieve anything by winning. When you are involved in football violence, you are constantly striving to improve the reputation of your firm. It gave us an excuse to put our differences aside and fight together; against whichever team we happened to be playing.

Bolton would have been a rough place even if the sport of football had never been invented. At the end of the day, would you rather we fought on a match day or beat seven shades of shit out of each other every weekend down at the local pub? Back in those days, I lived to fight. I fought the Spillamies, I fought the Scousers and I fought at the football. It was part and parcel of growing up in a place like Farnworth and violence has formed the basis for some of the closest friendships that I have made to date. The firm were bound together by our support for Bolton and we were about to show the rest of the country that we could hold our own against any firm that dared to stand in our way.

2
FROM THE STREETS TO THE TERRACES

To me football and hooliganism have always gone hand in hand, partly due the fact that there was violence at the first match I can remember attending. I was twelve at the time and my Uncle Jack and my cousin, Carol, had taken me to see a game against Luton in the 1972/73 FA Cup. It wasn't a good day for Bolton. We lost 1–0 and a load of Luton fans managed to sneak into the Lever End, looking to take our stand. They were hardly the most discreetly dressed bunch of people. They were wearing Clockwork Orange masks and bright-orange boiler suits. If they had opted for subtler clothing they might have got away with it but as it was they were spotted right away by an angry mob of Bolton fans, who chased them out of our end. I remember watching in awe from the back of the Burnden paddock as a horde of our lads followed them onto the pitch and set about them. We battered them, ran them back onto the terraces and then leathered them some more.

I was impressed by what I'd seen and I couldn't wait to see my friends from school so that I could fill them in on every last detail. From that moment on, I kept my eyes fixed firmly upon the Lever End at every game I went to. I was constantly on the lookout for the smallest sign of friction and I was always secretly hoping that something was going to go off. Watching the football was no longer enough to keep me satisfied. I wanted to see people getting their heads kicked in.

It was another three years before I became actively involved in the violence. I didn't have a great deal of choice either. I was stood in the

Lever End minding my own business when I suddenly realised that I was surrounded by a load of big, scary-looking fuckers that I'd never seen before. There were only eighty other lads from Bolton in there and I remember thinking, 'fuck me, something's definitely not right here'.

We were playing Chelsea and I had good reason to be apprehensive, because their firm had invaded our end and were just waiting for the right moment to get stuck in. All of a sudden, there was an almighty roar of 'Chelsea aggro' and it kicked off big style. I felt a volley of kicks and punches raining down on me from every direction and I scrambled down the steps, trying to get as far away from the mêlée as was humanly possible. I managed to clamber over the billboards at the front of the pitch but Chelsea kept pulling me back. They were punching me on the shoulders and twatting me in the back of my neck. I was shitting myself. I thought they were going to kill me.

Luckily, a copper got onto what was happening and he snatched me up off the pitch, just as I thought I was going home in a body bag.

'I haven't done anything,' I protested, worrying that he was going to arrest me.

'It's all right son,' he assured me. 'Your nose is bleeding, I just want to get it looked at for you.'

The Old Bill passed me over to the St John's Ambulance so that they could check me out. By this stage we were finally beginning to get the upper hand on Chelsea. Our reinforcements had arrived and lads were jumping over the turnstiles and climbing up on the roof to get inside the ground. It was just my luck. I had been right in the thick of it when we were getting battered but now that we were giving them a taste of their own medicine, I was waiting to get my nose seen to. I was missing out on the action.

'I'm off,' I told the medic.

I wasn't going to hang around and forgo a chance for revenge. The shoe was on the other foot and it was time for payback.

As I leapt back onto the pitch, I could see more and more of our lads making their way into the ground. If only they had been there ten minutes earlier, when I was getting beaten half to death. Some of the wall around the turnstiles had collapsed and there were hordes of Bolton supporters pulling the stones away and clambering in through the gap.

People were picking up the debris and launching it into Chelsea. The entire stadium quickly became a miniature battlefield.

Just as I was beginning to get stuck in to Chelsea's mob, I felt my hands being twisted up behind my back and a pair of handcuffs clicking shut around my wrists. This time I wasn't going to be carted off to the St John's Ambulance, I was properly under arrest. Back in the Seventies they would bollock you, give you a clip around the ear and tell you to fuck off home. Nowadays if you get caught fighting, the Old Bill will almost certainly haul you off to the station for questioning.

The copper took me outside the ground, gave me a boot up the arse and told me that I'd be in serious trouble if I tried to go back inside. One of my mates had been nabbed with me and he was on about waiting around after the game to see if anything else was going to kick off.

'You can get fucked,' I told him. 'I can't take any more of this. You can stay if you want but I'm going back to Farnworth.'

I was covered in blood, my head was sore and my back was killing me. I wanted to get as far away from the stadium as I possibly could. It had been a pretty fucking traumatic day. I had been arrested for the first time, taken my first proper kicking and experienced my first taste of real fear, all within the space of a couple of minutes.

My mum went off her head when she found out what had gone on at the match.

'You're grounded,' she told me. 'And don't think for one minute that you're going to go to the football again.'

I remember thinking, yeah right, you try and fucking stop me. I had discovered a world that was even more extreme than the one I already inhabited. From that day on, my life would never be the same again. I went to as many games as I could and fear quickly transformed itself into excitement. I can't even begin to describe the rush of adrenalin that you get when you're going toe to toe with another team's firm. It's the best feeling in the world and ever since my run-in with Chelsea's mob, I have been hooked.

3
PUNKS AND SKINS

If you're living a violent lifestyle, you need the right type of music to get you in the mood for a ruck. You can't put on an ABBA record and hype yourself up, you need something you can mob up and riot to. When I left school at age sixteen, bands like The Damned and The Sex Pistols had just started to enter the public consciousness and I was immediately attracted to their music. They were rebels, just like us, and they expressed their unwillingness to conform through their bizarre dress sense and their hard, uncompromising lyrics. While artists like the Village People and Lionel Richie were busy filling the charts with watered-down pop music, groups like Sham 69 and The Buzzcocks represented something that the average, working-class kid could relate to. Their music was full of the kind of energy and vitality that made you want to start a brawl. They made tunes you could row to, not the same clichéd love songs.

There was always fighting at the early punk gigs, especially when Slaughter and the Dogs were playing. They were one of my favourite bands, despite the fact that they hailed from Wythenshawe of all places. I suppose it stands to reason that a group from such a rough estate drew the type of fans who liked to put their fists up every now and again. Sometimes the entire crowd would be involved in the mayhem. I remember when they played at the Electric Circus[1] in Collyhurst

---

[1] The Electric Circus was the unlikely setting for the majority of Manchester's seminal punk gigs. Despite its less-than-glamorous location, The Buzzcocks, The Jam, The Clash and The Sex Pistols have all played there. A journalist for the *Bombsite* fanzine stated that the street the Circus was situated on 'looks like Hiroshima a while back' and went on to say that he 'Left the car two miles away . . . felt like staying with it.'

that a full-scale riot broke out. One minute the band was complaining about people throwing glasses onto the stage and the next thing, punches were being thrown right, left and centre. With songs like 'Cranked up Really High' and 'Where Have All the Bootboys Gone?' how could they have failed to elicit that type of response? Their gigs were pure adrenalin from start to finish. It was music to whip up a group of warriors into a frenzy the night before a battle.

Whereas most of the other patrons would accept that a bit of rowdiness was part and parcel of being a punk, there would always be one or two grumpy bastards who took exception to people banging into them. I remember when we went to see the UK Subs in Manchester and a load of Manc punks kicked off on us for knocking them about while we were pogoing. Fifteen of us ended up going at it with them at the front of the stage. Fuck knows how many of them were there but it felt like it was us against every fucker. The lead singer of the Subs was telling everyone to calm down but no-one was paying him any attention. I was holding my hand in towards my stomach because I had broken two of my fingers, which made people think I'd been stabbed. The bouncers must have been worried that I was badly injured because they let me stay inside the venue, even though I had been in the thick of the brawl. If they had known it was my fingers that were causing me so much pain, as opposed to my stomach, they would probably have chucked me out on my arse.

As well as fighting amongst ourselves, we were always getting into scrapes with the local teddy boys, who were bitter that we'd taken their shine away. They were the main men before we came on the scene and they weren't overly pleased about being last year's trend. The teds had the dress sense of the 1950s, whereas we were walking round with safety pins stuck in our ears and multicoloured Mohicans jutting out of our heads. Our conflicting dress codes led to clashes whenever our paths crossed.

I remember we were in the Queen's pub in Farnworth and a load of teddy boys turned up looking for trouble. They had been drinking heavily and were being a bunch of mouthy bastards, thinking that they were better than us because they had been around for longer. There were six or seven of us and forty of them, although to their credit half of them were trying to defuse the situation. We ended up giving them a right good hiding and they learned not to go about throwing their weight around. We may have been punks but most of us were football lads as well and none of the other subcultures were on our level when it came to violence.

The heavy rockers were even more hostile towards us than the teds. They thought that they were a cut above everyone else because they were into bands in which the singers could actually hold a note. They didn't seem to understand that punk was good *because* the singers couldn't sing. It was raw and unrefined, which was what made it so exciting. The rockers were a bunch of weirdoes who refused to mix with anybody who didn't have the same taste in music. We were always coming to blows with them for slagging punks off. They had a fair few bikers with them, who were usually up for a do. We may have listened to different genres of music but we were both fond of a good punch-up. It just goes to show you that even the most diametrically opposed groups can be brought together through their mutual love of fighting.

When there weren't any rows to be had, I kept myself occupied by singing in a band and DJ-ing at the Tuesday- and Sunday-night punk sessions at the Buzz Inn. Performing live gave me a different type of buzz. It was a way of releasing my pent-up frustration without the need for violence. I played at a couple of different venues and we recorded an eight-track demo at Flash Street Studios in Bolton. Our band was called Nervous Disorder and we had a mixture of different anti-police and anti-government songs. We were disillusioned at the direction the country was going in and our lyrics reflected that. Our style was hard, fast and aggressive and we embodied the punk mentality.

As well as playing our own original material, we did a punk version of the Rolling Stones song 'Jumping Jack Flash'. Our old guitarist Jimmy Ball has recently joined a punk cover band called Strangeways, which plays all the old punk songs, along with a bit of Oasis thrown in for good luck. They put on a first-rate show and if you ever get the chance to watch them live you should take it.

Nervous Disorder's first gig was at the Cyprus Tavern in Manchester city centre, which had a reputation for being a rough old pub. It was frequented by several different sets of football lads and stories were always circulating about what a moody venue it was. It couldn't have been as bad as people made out because we fucking destroyed the place. The minute we took to the stage, an angry crowd of punks forced their way into the bar and helped themselves to whatever they could get their hands on. By the time we had finished our set, the furniture had been smashed to pieces, the stage had been put through and there were gaping holes in the walls. It was certainly a night to remember and I don't think that you could have asked for a better introduction to our band.

After the gig, a couple of the staff tried to kick off with some of the punks who had gathered outside the venue. By this stage, everyone was as pissed as a fart and even the lads who didn't usually put their fists up were willing to have a go. It degenerated into a brawl and I couldn't help thinking that the night had gone as well as it possibly could have done. We had managed to whip the crowd up into a frenzy and the fact that the gig had ended in a mass street fight was the icing on the cake. I was buzzing my tits off and I couldn't wait for our next time on stage.

One of the reasons that our gig at the Cyprus went so well was that we took fifty local punks along with us. We were the only proper punk band in Farnworth, which meant that we could always rely upon our fellow townsfolk to turn out in force. As far as live performances were concerned, our only real competition came from a group from Little Lever, who had an Indian lad on guitar. It was rare to see black or Asian punks in those days, although the punk scene was always closely connected with the reggae scene. Most punks were into West Indian music and a lot of the Jamaicans were into bands like The Clash because they fused the two genres together.

Punks and skins are often portrayed as being right-wing, neo-Nazi types but the vast majority of the early punks were actually on the left. They were anti-establishment, which was what the country needed at the time, as we'd just had the Brixton riots and Maggie Thatcher was turning our country into a war zone.

I was quite politicised back in my punk days and I went on a few demonstrations. The one that sticks in my mind is the 1980 March for Jobs that me and Jimmy Ball did. We got a lift to Liverpool and walked to the Ford plant in Halewood, where we met up with a couple of other local punks and skins. Then, once we had everybody on board, we walked all the way over to Salford as a way of protesting about the lack of work.

The Salford Jets and the Naughty Boys were playing nearby so we decided to go and watch them while they were in town. The Naughty Boys were a well-known punk band from Wythenshawe and by sheer coincidence their guitarist was going out with my ex's sister. I knew him quite well and we had a lot in common, what with us both being into the same kind of music.

'How's it going, Dougie?' he asked. 'Have you still got your band?'

'Yeah,' I told him. 'We're still going strong.'

He had always been supportive of our music and he seemed genuinely interested in what we were trying to do.

'What's going on with you then?' I asked him.

'We're doing a gig at the university,' he told me, 'You're welcome to open up for us if you want.'

He didn't need to ask twice. I was straight on the phone to the rest of the band and they were all proper up for it. The next thing I knew, they were piling into a motorbike and sidecar and heading down to the uni with their instruments in tow.

Our support slot for the Naughties went down pretty fucking well and it's a shame the Salford Jets didn't play that day because we would have blown them out of the water. They were shit and it's always good to get a better reception than a big-name act. I loved doing live shows. The only downside to performing at punk gigs was the audience's habit of spitting at the bands. It was supposedly a sign of respect but you'd end up covered in phlegm from head to toe and it made me want to jump into the crowd and start banging people out. It was fucking disgusting and I don't know how the other groups put up with it. Saying that though, they probably didn't end up with as much spit on them because the crowd were going wild for us. I felt like I was seventeen-foot tall when I finally came off stage. Women were throwing their fannies at me right, left and centre and I got to tell a load of proper fit birds to fuck off so that I could go and have a pint with my mates.

My times with the band were some of the best experiences I have ever had, the only thing that has come anywhere close to the buzz of football violence. Although we only had a relatively low level of success, we felt on top of the world every time we did a gig.

Watching other people's shows could be almost as entertaining. I remember when I went to see The Damned at the Russell Club in Hulme, which was the club that Tony Wilson did his nights at before he moved them to the more famous Hacienda. The lead guitarist Captain Sensible came on stage butt naked and offered a pound to anyone who could provide him with a pair of underpants. I jumped on stage, ripped my undies off, passed them over and claimed my prize. I've never been shy of doing things like that, although I suppose the beer helped. The crowd was in hysterics and it was one of the funniest nights of my life.

After he had finished his set, Captain Sensible came across to where I was sitting and asked if I would like to go backstage and have a drink. My mates were proper envious. They were frothing at the mouth and yelling 'you lucky bastard'. I was rubbing it in and telling them that they should have jumped on the stage before I did and whipped their undies off.

The Captain was a sound, down-to-earth guy. He was off his fucking trolley but that was what made him such a first-class entertainer. The Damned are one of my all-time favourite groups and it was nice to know that they had a sense of humour to them.

As the years went by, popular music became cornier and cornier and, by the mid 1980s, the charts were dominated by shitty New Romantic bands, complete with weird haircuts, nail varnish and cheesy keyboard synths. The days of guitarists walking on stage stark bollock naked were long gone. Punk had shocked the masses and provided us with a means of venting our frustration against authority but, alas, it is no more. Nowadays people would prefer to listen to Britney Spears and Christina Aguilera rather than opting for something with a little bit more substance. Music has become commercialised and punk has been driven underground. It's a shame because there has never been another genre that's come anywhere close in terms of sheer energy. It's still the only thing I'll listen to and I'll always be a punk deep down, even if I don't dress like one any more. Give me Captain Sensible or Slaughter and the Dogs over the endless stream of manufactured pop groups that Simon Cowell manages any day of the week.

Whereas the likes of Johnny Rotten and Sid Vicious took great pride in dressing as unconventionally as possible, another highly influential movement of the Eighties revolved around doing the complete opposite. The punks and the skins were notable for their indifference to their appearance, whereas this new subculture was based around dressing in the top terrace fashions. Pringle and Lacoste labels replaced Mohicans and safety pins and a new generation of rebels was born.

Despite their conflicting dress codes, punk culture and casual culture were remarkably similar. Both modes of fashion sprang up as a means for the youth of the day to mark themselves out from the rest of society. Casuals clothing was just another way of going against the grain, as none of the other fans dressed that way. Fighting at the Electric Circus progressed to fighting on the streets and trashing pubs during gigs was replaced by trashing them on match days. Fashion has turned three hundred and sixty degrees and designer labels are now a counterculture in their own right.

4
BOYS, DRESSERS AND CASUALS

Before the term 'casual' was invented, lads who dressed in expensive forms of sportswear were referred to as 'boys'. They tended to be younger than your average, run-of-the-mill hooligans and they wore Adidas trainers, straight-leg jeans and Nike and Slazenger V-neck jumpers. They had wedge haircuts with the sideburns shaved off and, if it was a cold day, they could be found sporting green Peter Storm jackets. The lads who managed to get hold of these tops in any colour other than green were regarded as being at the cutting edge of fashion.

All the larger clubs around Manchester and Liverpool had their own boys and they would normally target other teams' boys, rather than going after your regular common or garden hooligans. The Old Bill didn't give them a second thought because they weren't your typical football lads. They were fresh-faced and innocent-looking and they tended to be left to their own devices.

As the years went by, more and more fans started dressing in terrace fashions. Pringle, Lyle and Scott, Lacoste and Fila became the order of the day, with Ellesse and Sergio Tacchini trailing closely behind. Trainers were also very important and Adidas Forrest Hills, Grand Slam, Nike Cortez and Diadora Borg Elite were all highly sought after. Those who chose to spurn their team colours in favour of the latest designer clothing were known as dressers. They weren't content with merely kicking the shit out of you; they wanted to do it in style.

Splits in the bottom of your bleached or stonewashed jeans were also considered trendy in the early 1980s. Dressing in your smartest clothes was a way of showing you were a cut above your rivals. The worst-dressed mobs would get the piss taken out of them and everybody else would call them scruffy cunts. We dressed similar to the cast of *The Firm*,[2] although none of us ever turned out in either an entirely yellow or an entirely red tracksuit. That must have been a Cockney thing.

In 1982, one of the most iconic pieces of terrace fashion made an appearance on the scene: the mighty Adidas Trimm Trab. Most people got them from a small store on the underground market in Manchester, just around the corner from the Roxy, where the punks bought their gear. You went into the stockroom, told them what you wanted, paid a £15 deposit and then you went back a week later to collect your trainers. There was only one shop in Bolton that sold them and they were pretty sought after.

Nikes and Reeboks were also a popular choice of trainers from 1982 onwards. Reebok had a factory shop at Bradley Fold just outside of Bolton, where you could buy new lines and seconds for a fraction of the shop price. Later, Ellesse and Sergio Tacchini came into fashion, along with anything else that featured at that summer's Wimbledon. Cerutti 1988 was another smart brand but it was quite difficult to get hold of and more expensive.

Bolton had a mob of around forty top dressers including a lad called Ian, who turned up at one of the home games wearing Trimm Trabs, bleached jeans with splits and a dark-blue jumper with a brown Giorgio Armani eagle. I remember taking the piss out of him and asking him why he had bought a Frank Bough[3] jumper. Little did I know that we'd all be wearing them a few months down the line.

Towards the back end of 1983, a couple of the smarter lads started wearing New Balance, mainly because some of the other brands were more readily available and they wanted something more exclusive. By this stage, Burberry, Aquascutum and Benetton were coming onto the scene and the range of different terrace fashions was gradually expanding and diversifying. Benneton rugby shirts were particularly

---

[2] A film based on the activities of London hooligans during the 1970s and 1980s.
[3] A television presenter from the Eighties who always wore Armani.

popular whereas Daks of London did a similar line that never really caught on.

Certain designer labels were slowly becoming synonymous with football hooliganism. By the time the year was through, every club in England had an associated firm of dressers. The 'boys' had graduated into men and the majority of football lads were now wholeheartedly embracing the casual dress sense.

In 1984, brands like HCC, Head and Berghaus appeared on the terraces. The Scousers were the first firm I can remember seeing in that style of clothing. They would bowl around in hiking boots, jeans and Head and Berghaus bubble coats, which was a relatively new way of dressing at the time. The look was just that little bit different and it soon caught on, which is more than can be said for the Mancs' attempt to bring flares back into fashion. They looked ridiculous and it just goes to show you that while some people are trendsetters, others don't have a fucking clue.

A year later, the *Sunday Times* ran a piece entitled 'Soccer Chic', describing how the 'soccer casual' was slowly taking over the terraces. From then on, 'dressers' suddenly became known as 'casuals' and everybody wanted a piece of the action. As hooliganism became more and more mainstream menswear replaced sportswear and Emporio Armani took over from Giorgio Armani. Football fashions were constantly evolving and progressing. Split jeans were soon a thing of the past and baggy jeans combined with three-quarter-length suede-and-leather jackets became the new in thing. What had originally been labelled a passing fad was proving to be an enduring and innovative cultural movement.

Henri Lloyd was one of the main brands to catch on during the mid 1980s and there was a factory outlet in Little Hulton where you could get it at a reduced price. Timberland was also becoming popular and shirts were now replacing T-shirts. The year of 1987 witnessed the rise of what is perhaps the single most iconic item of casual clothing to date: the Stone Island jacket. A shop in Manchester called Karl Twigs was one of the first places to stock them and they cost a whopping £400, which made them by far the most expensive item on the terraces. The compass badge on the sleeve was the Trimm Trabs of its day. It immediately marked you out as a casual and showed that you were willing to pay that little bit extra for your clothes.

Stone Island is still as popular today as it was then, although it is not as exclusive as it once was, for two reasons: too many snide imitations and the fact that you can buy it anywhere. The same goes for CP Company, which was the other main label to surface during that period. It was the brainchild of Massimo Osti, the man behind Stone Island, and provided us with the legendary CP Mille Miglia. A mate of mine bought a beige one for £700 during the early 1990s and I can remember telling him what a waste of money it was. 'It'll never catch on,' I warned him. I couldn't have been more wrong, as they're still selling for upwards of £400 even though they're nearly twenty years old.

The late Nineties saw the birth of another classic set of terrace wear in the form of CP Company's Urban Protection range. They came in a variety of different colours and sold for £800 each. They would have been cheap at half the price.

As we passed the millennium, Paul & Shark, Prada, MHI, 6876 and OTS all came onto the scene, closely followed by Barbour, Belstaff, Woolrich, Fjall Raven, Victorinox and Albam. Nowadays retro Eighties trainers are back in fashion, along with Clarks original desert boots and Mephisto rainbow shoes. A new brand called MA.STRUM is also becoming increasingly popular. Their clothing features a luminous compass badge similar to that of Stone Island and only limited numbers of each item have been produced.

Over the years, fashion has become an essential part of our identity. If we dressed like the regular, run-of-the-mill football fans then how would anybody know who we were? Certain brands are like a uniform and enable us to target other firms without accidentally laying into their scarfers. Casual wear is more than just a fashion; it's a way of demonstrating that you're up for it. If you dress like a hooligan then you get treated like a hooligan. It's as simple as that.

Nowadays casuals and hooligans are virtually synonymous and if you're a hooligan then it's a given that you'll dress in casual gear so that people know you're up for a fight. New brands are emerging every couple of months and the culture is more alive than it has ever been.

If you see a group of lads walking down the street dressed in their team colours then you know to leave them well enough alone. But if you see a bunch of game-looking bastards clad in terrace fashions you had better run for your fucking lives because the betting is that it's us.

So there you have it. We are not only one of the gamest firms in the country but we are also one of the best sets of dressers. With every new generation, a defining set of clothing emerges and we have done our best to keep up with the times. I have witnessed everything from Nike and Adidas to Prada and Armani hitting the terraces and have amassed a sizeable clothes collection along the way. What's the point in doing another firm over if you aren't going to look good doing it?

At the end of the day, we're a name-brand mob and only name-brand gear is good enough.

5
THE SCUM

Well I've told you how I grew up, what I listened to and what types of clothes I like to wear. Now all that's left is for me to introduce you to some of my all-time favourite fights. And what better place to start than with those twats Man U? Our loathing of those Munich cunts goes back a long way, to at least 1958, when their fans attacked our team coach near Wembley stadium just after the FA Cup final between the two teams.[4] That incident, plus an intense local rivalry, means that trouble is guaranteed every time we face them.

We harboured such an intense resentment towards them that in the run up to our home game against them on the fortieth anniversary of the Munich air disaster, in 1998, the authorities were worried sick that we would deliberately break the minute's silence. The Reds even mounted a campaign to have the match changed to another date.

'Anybody caught deliberately making a noise will be banned from the stadium for life,' warned a Bolton Wanderers official. 'The perpetrators will be easily identifiable by their seat numbers.'

Despite the threat of a lifetime ban, a lot of our lads walked out of the seats in disgust. The rest of the firm started singing Munich songs at the top of their voices.

'Yobs shatter silent tribute to Sir Matt,' wrote reporter Frank Wood in the *Bolton Evening News*. 'Morons . . . wrecked a minute's silence in memory of Sir Matt Busby.'

---

[4] Bolton won the final 2–0, thanks to a double from the great Nat Lofthouse.

I was having a shit at the time. I remember thinking to myself, 'Fuck the minute's silence, I fucking hate the scum.' I'm not a yob or a moron; I just really, really hate United.

Busby wasn't the only Munich who felt our wrath. A year earlier, the *Daily Mirror* had printed a story claiming that we had put a £10,000 reward up for anybody who was willing to attack Eric Cantona.

'We always deal with these situations as if the worst is going to happen,' stated Inspector Graham Robertson, one of the officers in charge of match security at Burnden Park. 'We are conscious that the nutcases have not gone away.'

First we were morons and now they were branding us as nutcases as well! The Old Bill even considered changing the route that the Reds team bus took to the game, using the logic that it might prevent us from kicking the Froggy bastard's head in. It was all a fuss about nothing because if somebody had put out a hit on Cantona they certainly never told me about it. I would have thrown in a tenner towards the costs.

Our hatred for the Reds is so intense that we have even taught our kids to hate them. All Bolton fans hate the bastards, not just our firm. The ill-feeling towards them has been handed down throughout generations and is currently stronger than ever.

One of our most memorable run-ins with the Munichs took place in 1975. It pains me to admit it but they got the better of proceedings and really leathered us. I'll let somebody else fill you in on the details because it hurts me to admit they've come out on top against us. Here is what one of our older lads has got to say about our crushing defeat at the hands of our bitter enemies the Reds.

Older lad

Our hatred for United started back in 1958, when Bolton played them in the FA Cup final. Because of the Munich air disaster, the rest of the country was rooting for them, which pissed us off no end. They were lapping up the sympathy and milking it to fuck, whereas they should have just got on with playing the game. We beat them 2–0 and our team coach was bricked by their supporters on the way to Wembley. From that moment onwards, we've been gunning for the cunts and our home game against them in March 1975 was the perfect opportunity for revenge.

Although I passionately detest them, Man U are the closest thing there has ever been to a super firm. They had thousands of lads with them even back in those days and they were running riot up and down the country. Countless articles about their escapades had been published in the national papers and I felt it was time for us to show them that we didn't care how well known they were. Bolton was looking to have a piece of them, regardless of their reputation. We may have had a smaller firm, but, at the end of the day, it's about the quality of your lads rather than the quantity. We had some proper nutcases turning out and we were going to do our best to leave them bloodied and broken.

On the day of the match, I headed into town fairly early on so as not to miss out on the action. I was shocked to see thousands upon thousands of Mancs, swarming all over Bolton. Most of the pubs in the centre were packed with the cunts. I couldn't see many of our lads about and the only ones that I did see were either being legged about the place or were keeping a low profile.

I somehow managed to make it to our regular boozer without getting my head kicked in, which was no small feat considering the amount of United that were milling about the streets. There were only around a hundred and thirty of our lads in there and there were a lot of nervous faces. Quite a few of our so-called hooligans had made their excuses and left, which was their loss really. Bolton versus Man U is about as intense a match as you can get and I was proper looking forward to it.

We stayed in the pub until 2.45 and then we headed to the ground en masse, tooled up to fuck and ready for war. Most of us had armed ourselves with glasses and bottles, although a couple were carrying knives and a lad called Big Kev had a small pickaxe hidden underneath his coat. It was time for us to teach those dirty Munich bastards a lesson.

On the way to Burnden Park, we bumped into a thousand-strong mob of United, walking nonchalantly along the Manny Road. Most of our firm scattered straight away but one lad wasn't at all fazed. Big Kev walked straight through United to talk to me, as if he'd been granted diplomatic immunity. He was a right crazy bastard! He was a really nice lad but I would be a barefaced liar if I told you that he wasn't a complete and utter lunatic.

The further we walked towards the ground, the more of their supporters there seemed to be. They were everywhere and groups of Bolton fans were getting turned over on nearly every street. A couple of our lads attempted to even up the odds by using weapons. One of them slashed a United supporter across the buttocks with a Stanley knife and another smashed a pint glass into one of the fuckers' faces. I can remember thinking, 'Good, I hope you fucking die you bastards!'

By the time we reached the stadium, the Old Bill were all over us. They were hitting out with their batons from every direction and a fair few lads got nicked. I decided to head off into the Lever End to avoid being either arrested by the coppers or kicked to fuck by the thousand-strong horde of Munichs that had gathered outside the ground.

United's end was a sight to behold. It was a swaying mass of red-and-white bodies and there must have been at least twenty thousand in there. It was fantastic to look at. I fucking despise them but I'll give them credit where it's due. It really was unbelievable.

There were only a couple of hundred of our lads in the Lever and a load of Munichs ended up taking it over. We were massively outnumbered by the cunts, which was fucking embarrassing seeing as it was our end. A couple of our older lads were plotted up next to a Warburton's advertising banner, throwing bricks at our rivals for the full ninety minutes, but the stubborn bastards were determined to stand their ground.

United ran us ragged in our own stand. I got punched in the nose part way through the game and a stream of blood spurted out all over my clothes, staining them a dark shade of red.

'Shit,' I thought, 'I was thinking of going out on Saturday night and I'm not going to be able to pull a bird with my nose bust open like this.'

You barely even realise that you've been hit at the time. It is only afterwards that the pain kicks in, once your brain has had the chance to register the injuries.

A couple of our supporters attempted to make a stand but being 100 per cent honest with you, we didn't stand a chance. United must have had at least two thousand lads with them, although saying that, this was back in the days when we were getting gates of thirty thousand-odd and we had no excuse whatsoever for our inferior numbers. You would have thought that the entire firm would have wanted to show their faces for a match like that. It just goes to show you that there are certain members of our mob who like to talk the talk without the ability to follow through on their words. If we had brought *a larger mob with us we might have stood a chance, but, as it was, we got totally humiliated.*

There were scuffles throughout the game and most of the Bolton supporters ended up taking their scarves off and leaving early to avoid a hammering. We got fucking leathered. A lot of our lads don't like to admit it but we really took a pasting. I felt embarrassed, humiliated and upset. I don't mind losing a fight but losing one to United is another story altogether. It took us months to get over our defeat, although I eventually got my revenge. I saw one of their firm at the local disco and threw him head first down a flight of stairs, as if to say, 'Have that you cunt, that's for taking our end.' He's a proper nutcase nowadays so I won't include his name.

Our battles against rival firms were always heated but when it came to Man U, we were looking to fucking injure them every time we played them. Bolton versus United was the pinnacle and I still get a shiver down the base of my spine just thinking about it. The only thing that has ever excited me more than the thought of the Munichs coming to Bolton was when there were rumours going around that they were stopping off in Farnworth before our game against them in 1995/96. I was literally rubbing my hands together.

Back in those days, the lads from Farnworth always stuck together, no matter what. There were a good few Man U and Liverpool fans in the town but if another football firm came down there we would all mob up on them. We were a tight-knit community and outsiders were looked upon with suspicion and disdain, especially in the case of the Munichs. Their proposed stop off was the talk of the town and we were waiting with bated breath for their arrival.

On the day of the match, I headed off down the pub fairly earlyish to discuss what was about to go down with the rest of our lads.

'I hope they do come down,' one bloke was saying. 'Bring it on. We'll do them Manc twats.'

We had some proper game faces with us at the time and we were fucking buzzing.

It got to around half one and there was still no sign of the Munichs so we decided to make a move. We were pissed off that they hadn't shown their faces and, to be honest with you, we were a little disappointed with them as well. Much as I hate Man U, I have always respected them and I had been looking forward to seeing how they would fare against the Farnworth lot.

'Come on lads,' I said to the rest of our firm. 'We can't wait around all day. Let's order ourselves some taxis to Bolton.'

I had got wind that a hundred and fifty of our lads had gathered in Bolton town centre and it was only a matter of time before they started going at it with the Mancs.

On our way to Bolton, one of our boys spotted some of the Mancs outside the Monteraze pub on Manny Road.

'Quick, stop the car,' he yelled. 'Let's get at 'em.'

The next thing I knew, we were piling out of the taxi and twatting them about the street.

There were little groups of Bolton and United going at it all the way to the ground. At one point, we chased a group of fifteen Munichs down the road only for another ten of them to come steaming into us at the hotdog stand, near the Rover showroom. We were on top of them for a while but more and more of the cunts kept turning up until we were eventually swamped.

Struggling against our rivals' superior numbers, we started backing off and then, just as we thought the situation couldn't get any worse, the Old Bill arrived en masse and chased us all the way up Weston Street. Luckily for us, a couple of the Moses Gate lads had gathered at the top end of the road. This added a few more boys to our squad and once the coppers had finally slung their hook, we were able to make our way back along the street and down the Manny Road towards the ground.

The plod were swarming about all over the place, wading into anybody who got in their way. They were batoning people right, left and centre, and although they will no doubt claim those tactics were necessary to keep the peace it looked pretty brutal to me. I have always thought they are a right bunch of heavy-handed cunts and they have certainly never been ones for subtlety.

After being chased around a bit by the Old Bill outside the stadium, we eventually ended up going in the Burnden Terrace and the minute I got inside the ground, I saw groups of rival supporters going at it in the Manny Road North End. Matches against Man U are heated at the best of times but this was set fair to be something special.

No sooner had I settled down to watch the match when I noticed a set of furtive-looking Mancs occupying the seats behind us. We tried to climb up the stand to get at them, but, luckily for them, the stewards promptly arrived on the scene and they were ejected from the ground before we had a chance to reach them. It was a shame because we were all proper up for it and the action before the game had got our juices flowing, ready for another confrontation.

The dirty Manc bastards ended up beating us 6–0. They wiped the floor with us, although that wasn't necessarily a bad thing as it had us hyped up for the post-match festivities. We had heard that the Mancs were getting escorted to the station in Moses Gate so we left the match a couple of minutes early to reduce the chances of the coppers getting onto us.

Despite our efforts to avoid them, the Old Bill ended up moving us up the Manny Road and keeping the Munichs a good five hundred yards behind us. There were a hundred rival lads there and we kept on trying to slow down so that they'd catch up with us but the plod weren't having any. They eventually engineered it so that United were on one side of the road and we were on the other, separated by a thick wall of coppers. Both firms were trying to get at one another but there were far too many OB on the scene for anything to go off.

By the time we had got to Moses Gate, there were coppers all over the place and it was looking increasingly unlikely that we were going to get a row. That is until one of the locals came bounding over to tell us there were fifty United holed up in a nearby boozer. One of our lads went steaming into their pub on his own to confront them only for their entire mob to pile out onto the pavement after him, kicking and punching him for all that they were worth. Well that was one way of luring them all outside, I suppose!

We charged across the road towards the pub entrance and another group of Mancs came running out of the train station to meet us. We tried our best to fend them off but there were far too many of them for us to cope with and just as we were beginning to back away, a load of Old Bill showed up. They legged us all over Moses Gate until we ended up round the side of St Peter's Way, near to one of the local primary schools.

By this stage, we were getting sick of being chased around the town by the coppers. It was all getting too much so we decided to head off back to Farnworth town centre via the back streets to prevent them from getting onto us. All around us, people were hurling bricks and pieces of debris into United's coaches and angry Bolton fans were throwing stones down onto the dual carriageway in the hope of hitting a car with a Man U supporter in it. It was difficult to remain low key in the midst of such a volatile atmosphere but we did our best to pass below the radar.

Once we had successfully made it back to Farnworth town centre, we spotted some Munichs stood outside the Black Horse pub and got straight into them. There were no Old Bill about and the Mancs were right in the heart of Farnworth, which really isn't where you want to be if you're a group of rival football lads. We fucking leathered the bastards. We beat the fuckers to within an inch of their lives and would have done a lot worse if the coppers hadn't shown up for about the millionth time.

'Time to make a move,' I sighed, as the Old Bill advanced along the street towards us, looking to crack our skulls with their heavy steel batons.

That was the end of it as far as I was concerned. I couldn't be arsed getting chased across the town again. It was time for me to head home. I've got to give the Munichs credit where it's due. They were brave enough to venture into Farnworth and they had some proper game lads with them. I can't fault the Mancs when it comes to their combat skills. I hate them but I rate them. They always bring an impressive mob with them and they aren't afraid to get stuck in.

Saying that though, when you've got as many supporters as United have, it gives you a bit of an unfair advantage over the other firms. Nearly all of our lads were from either Bolton or Farnworth, whereas a large proportion of theirs were from God knows where. Still, regardless of where their lads called home, they provided us with some stiff competition. Here's Phil to tell you about a run-in that he had with them a year down the line from the battle in Farnworth . . .

Phil

Man United are easily the most hated team in football but Bolton have always hated them even more than everybody else does. When I heard that we were playing them back in 1996/97, I was rubbing my hands together in anticipation of doing them.

There were minor clashes before the game kicked off but nothing particularly substantial. The real trouble started after the match had finished, when a group of Bolton lads followed the United lot to the Monteraze pub on Manchester Road and started laying into them. It went off big time and there were running battles all along the street.

After a couple of minutes of fighting, the Old Bill turned up and the United lads got off, which was a shame as we would have liked more time to get stuck into them. The coppers were surprised that it had gone off on the Manny Road, as they had been expecting the fighting to take place in Bolton town centre. They had been waiting for the trouble to start but they were clueless as to where it would kick off.

1997/98 was another season in which we had a memorable run-in with Man U. The new stadium at Horwich made it a little bit harder to front it but Bolton versus United was one of those games where nothing would have stopped it from going off. On the day of the match, I arrived at around two o'clock to see a thirty-strong mob of Reds outside the stadium, surrounded by Old Bill.

'Are they United?' a lad called Trevor asked me.

'It looks like it,' I replied. 'Let's go to the pub and tell the rest of our mob they're here.'

And off we went to the Barnstormers pub on Lostock Lane to rally the troops.

Thirty of our lot were drinking at the boozer and they were all proper up for it but there were so many OB around United that it was impossible to get at them. If the coppers didn't do one then it looked unlikely that we were going to get any action.

Although most of the lads had tickets, we decided to stay in the pub and watch the match on television rather than go into the ground. This proved to be a wise decision, because, about a quarter of an hour into the game, fifteen Man U lads walked through the door. Everyone went quiet. The atmosphere was tense as fuck and both sides knew that it was about to go off.

'What are you cunts doing in here?' one of our lot asked them. He already knew the answer, because as soon as the words left his mouth, he steamed into the new arrivals with his arms flailing everywhere. The United lads bolted towards the exit, leaving a handful of stragglers behind to take a hiding. They shouldn't have deliberately walked into a pub full of opposing supporters if they didn't want to get done.

The coppers arrived on the scene fairly quickly and ended up giving us the benefit of the doubt, as the Man U lads had come in with the intention of kicking off. The windows were broken and there were tables, chairs and bottles strewn across the floor but we were in the clear, as it wasn't us that had instigated the trouble. We stayed in the pub until around half four then we decided to move on to the Beehive on Chorley New Road.

Chorley New Road is in the perfect position for ambushing a rival team's firm. It's the road that fans go down after leaving the stadium, which meant that it wasn't long before our friends the Reds turned up. As soon as we got word that they had arrived, we all left the boozer and a lad called Danny spread his arms out and shouted, 'Come on, you Munich bastards!' We were outnumbered two to one so it was a crazy thing to do but that's Danny for you. He's always been a madhead.

The two opposing mobs charged at one another and a couple of blows were exchanged but the coppers were on the scene almost straightaway to try and put a stop to things. I had a court case coming up so I mingled in with the shirters to avoid getting nicked. I didn't want to end up with another charge on top of the one that I was already facing. I managed to get myself out of the way of the cops and stood back to watch the action from a distance. The Old Bill were pounding up and down the streets on horseback and the two sets of supporters were kicking the living daylights out of one another. The action continued for several minutes until the coppers finally managed to regain control.

United's mob ended up going in a pub called the Bridge Inn on Church Street and we went into the Black Bull, which was next door. Every time we left the boozer to have another go at our opponents, there seemed to be more and more Old Bill on the streets. At one stage, there were seven riot vans parked up at the side of the road. It looked as if it was going to be impossible to get another row with the Reds in the pub so we headed off into Horwich town centre to see if there were any United milling around there.

By the time we got to the centre, the action had subsided and nothing was going on. Oh well, I thought to myself, at least we got to have a ruck outside the Beehive. We didn't do too badly either. United had more lads than us but we stood our ground and nobody ran. We were badly outnumbered but we put up a valiant effort and, at the end of the day, that's what it's all about.

Although United usually had us outnumbered, there were a few occasions when the shoe was on the other foot. Our home game against them on 22 February 2003 springs to mind. We had far more lads with us but yet they still held their own and ended up doing okay.

At eleven o'clock on the morning of the match, a mob of Bolton lads got together at the Park Inn on Egerton Street and headed off to Stoneclough. We had heard that United's firm were plotted up there and we were looking forward to having it with them. However, by the time we reached our destination, the Old Bill had got wind of the Munichs and put them on a train back to Manchester.

The game was a 1–1 draw and as soon as the final whistle had blown, we made our way into the town centre to see if any Mancs were about. They had said that they would be back and we wanted to see if they had lived up to their word. Sure enough, we were sat around drinking our pints in the Clifton pub on Newport Street when word got round that a mob of Man U had arrived at the station. As their train pulled in, we piled out of the pub and headed over to greet them.

Fifty Reds were making their way across the platform when a hundred-odd Bolton lads showed up, looking for a scrap. We ended up going toe to toe on a flight of stairs. I was stuck at the back of the mob and couldn't really do that much. It was hand-to-hand combat at first but we didn't seem to be getting anywhere so we pelted them with stones, newspaper stands and bottles. The Mancs didn't budge an inch. They were game lads and they hung in there until the coppers turned up with their dogs. The civilians must have been wondering what the fuck was going on. They were running about the place, ducking for cover, and some of them looked terrified.

Quite a few lads got nicked but I was fortunate enough to get away and I slipped off for another pint at the Clifton. There were a fair few Bolton lads in there and they were covered in blood from the brawl.

The Old Bill hung about outside to prevent any further trouble from taking place. I remember feeling proud of our performance that day. There were eleven arrests, including one for possession of an offensive weapon, but I had managed to remain a free man and came away with some classic memories. The image of newspaper stands flying through the air is still fresh in my mind. It was a vicious battle and both sides did well.

The coppers are always proper on it whenever we go up against the Reds. When we played them on 29 January 2002, they locked United's lads in Corks pub on Bradshawgate and kept us in Yates's to ensure that nothing would kick off. There was a huge police presence between the two boozers but despite the Old Bill's best efforts to keep the situation under control, the Munichs managed to smash the windows of their pub from the inside. The police eventually brought in coaches from a local company, put United on them and drove them away.

We've had raging battles with United as recently as a year ago, and, although the police will always try their hardest to stop us, I can't see us packing it in any time soon. Some of our younger lads had a run-in with the Munichs in March 2010, proving that our passionate hatred of anything Red is still very much alive.

The battle between our youth and Man U was planned out in advance, when one of our younger lads lot got their contact number. Our lads had arranged to meet the United mob in Little Lever but one of the Reds rang and told them that they had gone to Radcliffe instead.

'We'll come to Little Lever though,' United's youth assured a leading younger Bolton lad.

They did show up but only to throw a bottle out of the window of a car. Some of our lads were in the New Inn pub and some were outside the Hardy Hall social club. They jumped into a car and gave chase but the United boys sped off down the street and we were unable to catch them. Just as the Bolton Youth were beginning to think that the Munichs were afraid to stand and have it with them, somebody shouted, 'They're here' and a brick came crashing through the window of the New Inn. Three Man U lads were stood outside, dressed from head to toe in black.

It was a thoughtless thing to do, as an innocent old woman ended up getting showered in glass as she sat and nursed her drink. The Bolton lads from the club and the pub sprinted across to punish the lads responsible. The terrified Munichs legged it across a patch of grass and an older lad from Little Lever caught up with one of them and gave him a kicking. Our younger lot caught another of the fuckers hiding in a garden hedge. He got the fucking shit kicked out of him. The so-called Men in Black should have turned a few more lads out rather than three of them showing up on their own. Maybe next time they will send their entire mob. Throwing things at us from a car and fucking off before we can have it is a coward's trick. They need to try a lot harder than that if they want to get a result.

We may have got the better of them on that occasion but we still have our work cut out for us whenever we play United. They are definitely one of the top five firms in the country and I've got a grudging admiration for them, despite the fact that I want them all to die. They're a bunch of dirty Munich bastards but they can't half fight.

Bolton will continue to despise United well into the future. We hate them with a passion and that's something that's never going to change, irrespective of the Old Bill's efforts to calm the situation down. They are glory-hunting wankers and no amount of dogs and horses are going to prevent us from showing them exactly what we think of them.

6
THE SCOUSERS

United may be our biggest rival but there is another set of supporters that we hate almost as much as the Mancs. They are the missing link between rats and people, human vermin that will steal anything that isn't nailed down. It's pretty fucking obvious who I'm talking about. They're from a city that's synonymous with crime and deprivation and they've got a firm that is synonymous with flashing knives around the place and attacking innocent scarfers. I am referring of course to the Scousers.

They are one of the scummiest sets of supporters that you're ever likely to meet but they can definitely have a row. I remember when we played them in the League Cup semi-finals in January 1977. I was only sixteen and I travelled down there in a van with eighteen older Farnworth lads. There were over fifteen thousand Bolton fans at Goodison that night and it went off all over the place. We were able to have a pop at our rivals before and after the game, and, to our credit, there aren't too many firms that will go there looking for it like we did.

The second leg at Burnden Park was an equally charged affair. By the time we had arrived at the ground, the Embankment End was already three-quarters full and a raucous chant of 'Bolton aggro!' was resounding round the stadium. Darts, coins, nuts and bolts were flying all over the place and the atmosphere was proper tense. We lost 1–0 in the end and that was the end of my Wembley dream. I was pissed off, as were the rest of our lads, and the Scousers weren't exactly modest about their victory. They were crowing their fucking arses off, singing

Wembley songs at the top of their voices and winding us up into a state of frenzy.

As soon as we got outside, we mobbed up on the car park and right along the Manny Road, ready to attack our opponents the second they left the ground. Minutes later we were running the cunts along the street as the sound of sirens, barking dogs and breaking glass mingled with their screams. A couple of the Scousers got chased into the churchyard opposite the station and we ran in after them. We booted fuck out of them and one of them started trying to climb a nearby tree in a desperate attempt to get away. The rest of our lads grabbed him and pulled him back and one lad tried to hang him by his scarf while another set fire to it. Their poor guy was terrified and just as I thought it couldn't get any worse for him somebody started poking lit cigarettes into his face. He was screaming his head off and I thought that it was all a little bit out of order so I decided to head off back to Farnworth.

Once I got to Farnworth, I met up with a couple of our older lot and filled them in on what they had missed.

'The rest of our mob caught this Scouser and they were stubbing cigs out on his face,' I told them. 'It was over the top, if you ask me.'

The next thing I knew, one of the older lads had given me an almighty crack and I was on my arse.

'You need to wake the fuck up and stop your whingeing, you little cunt,' he told me. 'That Scouse wanker would have slashed any one of us if he got the chance so what are you complaining about?'

Well, that was me told. He was right as well, although I still wouldn't have wanted to be in the Scouser's shoes. That poor bastard got fucking terrorised, as did the rest of his fellow Evertonians. One of our older lads was there to witness some of the things that I missed. He was lucky enough to see a fair few rival lads getting the beating of their miserable, bin-dipping lives. Here's his version of the night's events . . .

Older lad

It was a Tuesday-night game and we mobbed up early in Trotters, ready to get stuck into the Scousers. We must have had a good six hundred lads out and by half six, the Alma Inn, the Prince Bill and the Balmoral were filled to the brim with Bolton. Rumours were circulating that a Scouser had been thrown through the window of the Swan and I had a feeling it was going to be a game to remember.

At quarter to seven we left the pubs and made our way to the corner of Bradshawgate, where we waited for the football special to come into the station. Sure enough, at seven o'clock, a horde of marauding Scousers piled out of the entrance and came down Trinity Street towards us. We waited until they got to the corner of Manny Road and then we charged straight at them. They immediately panicked and scattered in every direction. The night was still young and we had already got them on their toes.

A fair few Scousers got caught and kicked to fuck and one or two of them ended up getting stabbed. We had them running around the place like a mob of headless chickens and it seemed as if the action went on for fucking ages before the coppers regained control. Everton were eventually placed inside an escort and walked all the way to the ground. We closely shadowed them the whole way there and you could see the fear in their eyes. We were pelting them with bricks and bottles and a couple of our lads even managed to run through the line of coppers and get stuck into them.

Inside the ground, there were missiles being thrown back and forth, which led to a fair few people needing treatment from the medics. We lost 1–0 in the end and we were fucking gutted. That was our chance of going to Wembley well and truly scuppered.

After the game, hundreds of us massed up on Manny Road, angered by our defeat. The Scousers seemed oblivious to our rage and the minute they were let out they started singing 'Wembley, Wembley'. We couldn't have asked for a better excuse to get stuck into them. As we charged along the road, their gleeful crowing was replaced by a chant of 'Bolton aggro, Bolton aggro'. They fucking shat themselves. The dirty bastards were straight on their toes and one of them tripped, stumbled and ended up getting stabbed. We chased them all the way up to the station, where they jumped the barriers to get away from us.

The Scousers were a sorry sight that night. They went home bloodied and broken and I even heard a rumour that one of them was stabbed in the head with a chisel. It was probably the worst kicking I've ever seen any firm get at Burnden Park. They will no doubt think twice before boasting the next time they win at Bolton.

Truth be told, that particular game wasn't your typical run-in with the Scousers. They normally aren't so easy to turn over. We have had a fair few fearsome battles with them throughout the years. Here is Phil to fill you in on his encounter with them a couple of decades down the line . . .

Phil

The Everton lot certainly weren't shy and they had that natural Scouse naughtiness bred into them. I'm not going to lie to you, it's always scary going to their ground and it might not even be their football lads that end up doing you in. There's always plenty of the local scallies waiting around the stadium, looking for a row.

Home games against the Scousers could be just as naughty as away games. One hundred and fifty of them would have no problem whatsoever with travelling into somebody else's town, looking for a ruck. It was during our game against them at Burnden Park in 1995/96 that the bin-dippers really showed me what they were capable of. We were sat about drinking our pints in Trotters and the Alma Inn when the noise of police sirens and heavy footsteps alerted us that something was going on. A couple of our lads rushed over to the windows to see what all the commotion was about and they were confronted by the sight of a horde of marauding Everton fans, swarming towards the pub.

The coppers had the bright idea of stationing a police horse in front of the door to Trotters so that we were trapped inside. Angry groups of Scousers were hurling bricks and bottles into the windows of the pub but everything they tried to throw at us was bouncing off the thick wire mesh that covered the glass. There was a monstrous amount of Old Bill there and they quickly managed to get the bin-dippers back under control, shepherding them further along the road so that they were unable to do the boozer any more damage. Then, when the Scousers were a fair distance away, the police horse trotted away from the exit and a swarm of eager Boltonians piled out onto the streets.

The Scousers eventually managed to navigate their way around the coppers to the Wagon and Horses, looking to have a go at the occupants. The pub was proper crowded and a couple of our lads were stood outside supping their pints, which was handy as it meant that they were able to act as unofficial spotters.

'They're here,' came a frantic voice from just outside the pub, quivering with a mixture of fear, excitement and nervous anticipation. 'The Scousers are here. Let's get into them.'

We were walking down the Manny Road surrounded by Old Bill when it first kicked off.

'Fuck this,' I thought to myself, 'I'm having a piece of this, coppers or no coppers.'

Before I knew it, I had gone tearing across the road into their mob and I was scrapping away like there was no tomorrow.

There were running battles all the way to the ground and by the time we arrived, there were so many people going at it that we didn't know which side was which. It was a gigantic free for all, with people punching and kicking anybody they didn't immediately recognise as being a member of their firm. The coppers had completely lost control and it was bordering on a full-scale riot. We ended up brawling away at the back of the Burnden Paddock, dodging projectiles right, left and centre and loving every single minute.

The sheer unpredictability of the situation had me tingling with excitement. Bricks and bottles were flying about all over the place and one of our lads got hit in the face with a rock. When a mate takes a pasting like that, it spurs you on to fight that little bit harder. In the heat of the battle, you haven't got time to be afraid. It's only when it's all over and done with that you've got the opportunity to sit back and reflect on the risks you've taken. I eventually managed to make it inside the ground relatively unscathed. I had a couple of cuts and bruises but it was a miracle that I hadn't ended up going home in an ambulance.

Just as I was beginning to think that the action had momentarily subsided, I noticed a brave bunch of Scousers, scrapping away in the Great Lever stand. Missiles started flying about the place again and the entire stadium descended into uproar. Bricks were sailing through the air and injuring people all over the shop and the atmosphere was tense as fuck.

The game ended in a 2–2 draw, which helped to defuse the situation to an extent, because if there had been a winner the losing side would have gone ballistic. I was slightly disappointed, as I'd been hoping for another battle but, by this stage, police reinforcements had been drafted in and there were far too many coppers on the scene for anything to go off.

Everton did themselves proud that day. They're not the type of firm that will travel to another team's city only to spend the whole time hiding. They're from a rough neck of the woods and you can definitely see it in them. Whereas the Bolton Old Bill were probably proper relieved that nothing had kicked off after the match, I can remember feeling gutted. It would have been the perfect end to the perfect match if we had been able to have one last go at them before the day was over.

So there you have it, although we might have run the Scousers ragged during our semi-final with them, they are anything but a walkover. They've got some game lads with them and they like their tools as well. They breed them rough around those parts and they can certainly hold their own. Now all they've got to do is stop slashing innocent shirt-wearing football fans and quit going through the bins and they might get our respect.

7
THE EDL CONNECTION

Okay so we hate the Mancs and we hate the Scousers but does our hatred extend from rival teams to different ethnic groups? Over the years Bolton are a team that have been marred by accusations of racism but where do you draw the line between taking the piss and exhibiting a genuine prejudice? Every firm worth speaking of has a small far-right contingent within its ranks but they're usually in the minority. The truth is that most of our lot couldn't give a fuck about race. We've had a couple of black and Asian lads with us over the decades and we have always treated them with respect.

The claims that Bolton are a racist team go back to the late 1980s, when our fans would lob bananas onto the pitch as a way of winding the black players up.

'I was not at the . . . game but I am told one or two bananas were thrown,' Superintendent Brian Swayles told the *Bolton Evening News* after our home game against Blackpool in 1988. 'This is not funny. It is disgusting behaviour which brings shame on the borough.'

What Mr Swales neglected to mention was that we had telly programmes like *Till Death Us Do Part* and *Love Thy Neighbour* at the time and racial slurs were still commonplace. Our behaviour was typical of the attitude of society as a whole. Making fun of somebody because they were a different colour was generally more acceptable.

Then there's the whole English Defence League connection. Nowadays a lot of our lads are affiliated with the EDL. Their demonstrations are also a really good platform for networking. Whenever I go to an EDL event, I always come away with phone numbers for various different mobs from up and down the country.

Rather than being the divisive, race-hating organisation that the media make it out to be, the EDL has had a unifying effect on football lads. It has brought together mobs that wouldn't have given each other the time of day prior to its existence. Our younger lads never thought they would end up being mates with Stoke but they have befriended a couple of members of their firm at the demonstrations and the animosity that existed between our firm and theirs has been significantly eroded.

A lot of the lads that have been banned are using the EDL as an alternative to the matches now that there are so many hooligans attending the events. The media claim that the EDL is the modern-day equivalent of the National Front but that is bollocks. It is simply a response to the Muslim extremists who were heckling our troops as they paraded through Luton after their return from Iraq in March 2009. With cunts like that going around stirring up trouble, can you really blame us for taking to the streets? We've got nothing against your average, run-of-the-mill Muslims. It's the radicals that we don't like and the EDL is our only means of expressing our disgust at what they're doing to our country. I believe wholeheartedly in what the organisation stands for and I think that the media have branded us as racists without taking the time to examine what we are about.

This extract, from a *Daily Mail* report on the Manchester EDL demo in October 2009, is typical.

> Some of the men hide behind balaclavas, others wear black hoodies. A few speak on mobile phones, their hands pressed against their ears to block out the cacophony. These are some of the most violent football hooligans in Britain and today they have joined together in an unprecedented show of strength. Standing shoulder to shoulder are notorious gangs – or 'firms' as they are known – such as Cardiff City's Soul Crew, the Bolton Wanderers Cuckoo Boys and Luton Town's Men In Gear. . . . There is talk of the need for a 'street army' and there are links with football hooligans and evidence that violent neo-Nazi groups including Combat 18, Blood and Honour and the British Freedom Fighters have been attending demos.

Flattered as I am that they ranked us amongst the 'most violent football hooligans in Britain', their attempts to paint the EDL as racist are laughable. Our doors are open to anybody, irrespective of their racial or religious background, just so long as they don't attempt to impose their views on us. Our gripe is with the scumbags who noisily disrupt soldiers' funerals and attempt to get Sharia law established in our courts. We've got our own fucking law so why should we change it for them? It has worked well for thousands of years.

Rather than demonstrating their support for our cause and proving their opposition to the radical element in their midst, certain members of the Asian community want to kick off with the EDL whenever they get the chance. It's funny how they hardly ever rate a mention in the papers, whereas we are constantly demonised and labelled violent and disruptive. During our rally in Bolton on 20 March 2010, a big fuck-off mob of them turned up looking for a ruck but the Old Bill seemed intent on targeting us. It was yet another example of the EDL being painted as the bad guys and the real troublemakers being let off scot-free.

On the day in question, a couple of Bolton lads had gone in a local boozer before it was officially open and somehow managed to get served. The rumour is that the landlord was so scared of them that he allowed them to buy some drinks, despite the fact that the pub was still being cleaned. This was at around 8.30 a.m. and, by 10.30, there were a few hundred EDL supporters in there, all hoping to get a couple of early pints in before the demo kicked off. Lads from Luton, Mansfield, Preston and the Midlands mingled with the hordes of Cuckoo Boys who had turned out to show support for the English way of life. The Old Bill were completely oblivious to us, focusing instead on the droves of EDL arriving via minibus, coach and train and herding them all together in a car park near Shiffnall Street.

By the time the coppers had got onto us, there were fucking hundreds of us, both inside and outside the pub. The OB completely surrounded the boozer with riot vans and arranged for coaches to take us to the car park. Meanwhile, two coach loads of West Brom had turned up at a pub in Walkden and a mob of Chesterfield had met up with the lads from Little Lever at another location. People were coming from far and wide to voice their discontent.

When the coppers finally decided to take us to the demo, forty of us managed to give them the slip and went in Durty Gurtys bar to get a couple more pints in. There were some Bolton lads, some Blackburn lads and some Mansfield lads already in there and they told us there were 150 Asians on the outskirts of the town centre, kicking off with everybody. And we're the troublemakers? Give me a fucking break.

After we had drunk our fill in Gurtys, we left the bar and made our way up Bradshawgate. We were looking for another boozer but all the pubs were shut so we headed up to the top of Bank Street instead, where we met up with a few of our younger lads.

'Pepper Alley is still open,' one of the younger lot told me. 'It's full of Bolton lads and there's a fair few Blackburn and Mansfield in there as well.'

It sounded like as good a place as any to get a couple more pints in before the demo.

Pepper Alley was packed with EDL and word soon got round that a mob of Asians was kicking off near McDonald's. It was time for us to show them that we were unwilling to sit back and let them bully our supporters. You can't hold a peaceful protest when a group of people turn up with the sole intent of causing trouble. The only option left was for us to kick the fuckers' heads in.

We piled out of the boozer and made our way over to Maccy D's, where a load of angry-looking Asians were bouncing around the streets, looking to flare it off. We were bristling in anticipation of a row but just as we were about to get stuck in, a load of Old Bill came charging across to stop us, including a couple who were on horseback and a few with dogs. Some of our lads got nicked for fuck all and the rest of us headed off back to Pepper Alley, not wanting to spend a night in the cells.

The staff at Pepper Alley refused to serve us so we decided to try our luck at the Queen Elizabeth on Fletcher Street. By this stage, the Old Bill were stuck to us like leeches and it looked as if our chances of having a ruck were well and truly scuppered. Then, as we were walking across Sainsbury's car park, we saw a massive mob of Asians a couple of hundred yards up the road, near to the casino. 'Game on,' I thought. 'Let's get into them.'

Unfortunately for us, a load of Old Bill hurried onto the car park to prevent anything from going off. We were forced to continue on our journey towards the Queen Lizzie, as we didn't want to risk getting nicked. The boys in blue were fucking everywhere and a few of our lads got stopped. A couple of riot vans eventually appeared and we had to take a detour down an alleyway leading towards Lever Street. It was a foolish move, because there was another van at the other end of the alley and we were penned in for a stop and search. One of the lads got arrested for some kind of petty misdemeanour and ended up with blood all over his head. I think he must have been done in with a baton.

As it turned out, we had wasted a lot of time and effort. The Queen Lizzie was closed and we were left standing around the place, wondering where to go instead. Then, just to make matters worse, the Old Bill showed up en masse and all but three of our firm disappeared into a nearby housing estate to avoid getting hassle. Me and the two other lads who had stayed outside the pub decided to make our way back to Pepper Alley and that was it for us. Not much else went on, although our younger lads knocked about all night, getting up to all kinds of mischief.

The plod were all over us that day, whereas the Asians received a fraction of the attention. The same thing happened in August 2010 at our Manchester demonstration. The coppers were quick to get stuck into us and several of our lads ended up going home covered in truncheon marks.

The Manchester demo drew support from all over Britain. Between nine and eleven that morning, lads from Blackburn, Preston, St Helens, West Brom, Luton and Cardiff gathered at the York pub on Newport Street in Bolton. The plan was for us to meet up there and get the train to Manchester Piccadilly station once we'd got a couple of drinks down the hatch. Some of the Bolton lads set off early to avoid getting boxed in and treated like shit by the Old Bill but by the time the majority of us had left the pub, the streets were filled with plod.

Upon arrival in Manchester, we were greeted by yet more coppers, who kept us in the station for a good half hour before escorting us to the demo site at Piccadilly Gardens. The majority of the people that we walked past on the way there seemed to support the EDL, although the Old Bill definitely didn't. They were heavy-handed as fuck and kept lashing out with their batons for no reason. They weren't the only ones who were intent on giving us a hard time either. A big group of anti-EDL troublemakers had gathered in a side street to our left and they were hurling abuse at us. They were a mix of United Against Fascism wankers and local Asians who were looking for a fight.

We managed to restrain ourselves from attacking the rival protestors until one of them threw a missile at us. That was it. They had crossed the line. Did they expect us to stand there and take that shit? Fuck that. It was time to teach the cunts a lesson so we charged across to do them. The coppers weren't having any of it and they whacked us back in the direction that we had come from with their batons. Some of our lads ended up getting batoned onto the pavement, which seemed to get the Old Bill's goat.

'Get off the footpath,' an angry copper screamed, flailing wildly with his truncheon.

Meanwhile, two of his colleagues had one of my mates on the floor and they were smacking him all over his legs. I grabbed their struggling victim and tried to pull him back into the road, prompting them to turn on me. They started twatting me on my thighs but despite their attempts to prevent me from intervening, I somehow managed to get the lad to safety before they could do him any more harm.

When we reached the site of the demo, the coppers crammed us behind a six-foot metal fence, whereas the UAF lot were allowed to come and go as they pleased. They had us caged in like a bunch of animals and they wouldn't even let us out for a piss. To make matters worse, the coppers were deliberately getting in people's faces. They were bringing their dogs right up close to provoke a reaction and a couple of unlucky lads ended up getting bitten to fuck and then arrested for no reason. What were the charges going to be – failing to provide a substantial enough meal for the Old Bill's pets?

Eventually the demo kicked off but nobody could hear the speaker, what with all the noise. The soap-dodging UAF scum were kicking up a racket and successfully ruining our event. They were an eclectic mix of tree-hugging students, PC-obsessed extreme left-wingers, trade unionists and up-their-own-arse local MPs. They couldn't even keep their mouths closed during the two-minute silence for our lost heroes from the armed forces. A disgraceful, big-mouthed female politician was shouting, 'Scum, scum, scum!' for the full duration, which caused us all to shout back and wound the Old Bill up to swing their batons about some more.

The coppers drove us all back against the fence until there was nowhere left to go and then laid into us with their dogs. The lads at the front of the group got savaged and when we were eventually allowed to leave we were made to wait while they took us out two at a time. As we were herded across the city centre towards Victoria station, the UAF continued to wind us up, spitting at us and throwing a volley of missiles in our direction from behind a row of fencing. The Old Bill didn't even tell them to stop, never mind nicking them. To me it was clear from the outset whose side the cops were on.

Bar the UAF and the Asians, most of the people on the streets were eager to register their approval for our cause. It was good to see that the UAF hadn't managed to turn the general public against us. Young and old alike were demonstrating their support by clapping their hands as we went past, which helped to draw the sting from the way that the coppers had treated us.

By the time we reached the station, I was dying for a pint and in desperate need of a cig.

'I'm not standing on a patch of grass for nearly four hours ever again,' I said to one of my mates. 'Fuck that.'

A lot of the other lads agreed, although once we had got back to Bolton and got a couple of beers down our throats, we soon changed our minds. We ended up eagerly discussing the next EDL event, which was to be held in Leeds. Like fuck the heavy-handed coppers and UAF hippies were going to prevent us from turning up. Nobody else dared to speak out against the spread of militant Islam for fear of being labelled racist so it was up to us to defend the British way of life.

The powers that be had tried their hardest to break our spirit and had fallen flat on their arses. But it wasn't only the English police that attempted to prevent us from holding demonstrations. When we went to a joint English Defence League–Welsh Defence League rally in November 2009, the Taffy Old Bill were just as eager to get rid of us. They started off by turning up at the pub that we were drinking at on the outskirts of Wrexham town centre and continued to make things difficult for us throughout the day.

The OB shoved us on a coach and dropped us off outside the Elihu Yale pub on Regent Street. There were a fair few Wrexham lads about the place and a couple of them tried to have a pop at us. We pushed forwards against the line of plod that separated them from us, prompting the coppers to start laying into whoever they could get their hands on. One of the Wrexham lads ended up getting nicked and we were quickly surrounded by Old Bill and escorted back to our coach.

'You can't stay here any more,' a copper told us. 'You're going to have to leave the town.'

We hadn't even been there for a full hour and we were already being forcefully ejected. The Old Bill followed our coach out of Wrexham all the way to Frodsham, a small semi-rural town between Warrington and Chester, where we piled off the coach and into the Bear's Paw pub. We got a couple of drinks in there and headed over to the Golden Lion, which was directly across the road.

Most of the boys can usually handle their drink but one of our older lot could hardly stand up and caught the attention of the landlady, who went mental. We later found out that our lad's nephew had been spiking his drinks all day. At the time, it caused him a lot of hassle but he is able to look back and laugh about it now.

We eventually moved on to a pub called the Cholmondely Arms, which was just down the road and round the corner, near to the town square. We were sitting there drinking our pints when the OB turned up and told us to leave the town. It was fucking unbelievable. It was the second town that we'd been kicked out of in a single day. The coppers were a bunch of wankers and ended up nicking one of our lads for fuck all. We were going mad, telling them exactly what we thought of them.

'If you don't leave now, your coach is going to go without you and a lot more of you will get arrested,' we were told.

Knowing when to admit defeat, we piled back inside the coach. The coppers had won. We were left with little choice but to head off back to Bolton, minus the lad they had hauled off to the station, who was released the following morning with an £80 fine.

'A PROTEST against Islam by the English Defence League spilled over into Frodsham and led to an arrest,' Paul Mannion notes in the following Thursday's *Chester Chronicle*. 'Before things got out of hand an army of police officers waiting outside the pub asked the group to leave, before arresting a twenty-year-old from Bolton for being offensive to the officers.'

Well I guess if protesting about being chucked out of the town for no good reason counts as 'being offensive' then he was guilty as charged.

We have been kicked out of a couple of places while supporting the EDL. Our demonstration in Leeds in October 2009 ended up with us being forcefully ejected from Manchester on the way back. The Old Bill were swarming all over us the minute we entered Leeds, searching us one by one and keeping us in the station for almost an hour. Once the coppers had finally let us out, we met up with a mob of Leeds, Middlesbrough and Darlington lads and made our way over to the square where the demo was being held. The UAF were holding a counterdemonstration nearby and a load of EDL managed to get past the Old Bill and made their way towards them. They were met by yet more plod, who forced them back the way they came. However, during the action, six of us managed to walk into a shopping mall and slip out into the city centre. Like fuck we were going to let the coppers tell us where we could or couldn't stand.

We had a bit of a walkabout and found a pub up a narrow little walkway, out of the way of the Old Bill. Once we were safely inside, I got on the phone to the lads and started giving them directions to the boozer. There were already a couple of Leeds lads in the beer garden and dribs and drabs of Bolton made their way over until we numbered around thirty.

We eventually moved on to another pub, had a couple more drinks and then headed back to the station. Part way through our journey, we saw a group of Rochdale lads wandering about the place and one of them tried to get lippy with us. A Bolton lad came very close to slapping him but, luckily for him, there was a load of Old Bill around. Had they not been there, he would have almost certainly got a kicking.

When we got to the station, some of the lads started pissing around and having a laugh, at which point a copper singled one of them out and told him he wasn't getting on the train.

'Don't worry,' we assured the lad. 'We'll all pitch in to get you a taxi to Dewsbury and then we'll get off the train and meet you there. Whilst you're waiting for us to get there, you can find a decent pub.'

We ended up stopping for a couple of beers in Dewsbury, with the Old Bill still hot on our case, and then we got back on the train and continued on our journey. Once we had arrived in Manchester, we left the station and went for a beer at one of the pubs just down the road. We were sat outside the boozer drinking our pints and having a bit of a laugh when our good friends the OB came striding over and told us to drink up because we were heading back to Bolton. Once again, the coppers had moved us on for no real reason other than the fact that we were being a little boisterous.

As we were finishing our drinks, a group of lads walked past and somebody called them Mancs, which didn't go down too well. They were apparently from Stockport, which is on the edge of Cheshire, and they were similar to us in that they didn't like people confusing them with Mancunians. We stood up and they immediately backed away. They were all mouth.

'Right that's it,' chimed in a meddling Old Bill. 'Time's up, you're all off back to Bolton.'

A couple of minutes later, a load more coppers turned up and we were escorted to the station. It was time for us to call it a day. I wonder, do you think the UAF would have received the same treatment? I think not.

Our Nottingham demonstration in December 2009 was yet another occasion when the coppers tried to ruin things for us. We had planned to pick a couple of Wrexham lads up at Stoke on the way down but the Old Bill turned up just before they arrived.

'Where are you going?' they grilled us. 'What are you doing here?'

As if we needed to explain ourselves to them. We weren't doing anything illegal so I can't see what their problem was. We were meant to be heading off to Derby to meet up with some more lads but the coppers were having none of it. They made our coach driver take us straight to Nottingham, which was a pain in the arse.

Once we got to Nottingham, we piled out of the coach and into the Company Inn on Canal Street, where we had arranged to meet the rest of the EDL. The pub was pretty full and there were a load of people stood outside as well. Arsenal, Bristol, Luton, Wolves, West Brom and Cardiff were all out in force and we were chatting with lads from all over the country for a good hour.

The Old Bill eventually ushered everybody out of the boozer, ready to take us to the demo. They shoved us all into an escort and started walking us over to Nottingham Castle, where it was set to take place. A couple of lads managed to break away but the majority of us had no choice but to comply with the coppers' wishes. They had us completely surrounded.

As we pressed on towards the demo, the OB did their usual routine of baton-charging us about the place on their horses and getting up close to us with their dogs. One lad lashed out in frustration and kicked a police dog. It had been going round biting people and he was fed up with being attacked. He was mauled to fuck and ended up screaming at the top of his lungs for the coppers to rein the fucker in. They pulled the savage beast back but rather than apologising to its victim for allowing the dog to tear his legs to shreds, they proceeded to arrest him. What a bunch of cunts.

The Nottingham constabulary could definitely do with altering their tactics. It goes without saying that if you constantly treat somebody like shit then they are eventually going to snap. They were pushing and shoving us around the place and hitting people with batons, making it clear that they didn't want us to have a peaceful demonstration. At the end of the day, our shitty government doesn't want the EDL to get any bigger so they try their best to make life difficult for us. It's funny how none of this ever happens when extremist Muslims are poppy burning and slagging off our troops. Double standards, anyone?

When we got to the castle, one of the lads spotted the Bolton football-intelligence officers up on the walls, videoing us. The Wolverhampton football intelligence were there as well. If I didn't know better, I would have thought that it was a Wolves versus Bolton game. Surely the cunts had something better to do with their time. But, then again, if they didn't have enough to do then they might have been out of a job and it is quite a cushy little number supervising us. They get to go to the matches and attend the EDL demos and if the team they are assigned to gets into Europe then they get an all-expenses paid trip abroad.

The minute the demo had finished, the Old Bill started pushing us again and I ended up on my arse. My legs got trapped under a crowd of people and by the time my mate had pulled me up, I was proper sore and bruised. The coppers were making things extremely unpleasant for us.

Frustrated at the way that we were being treated, our younger lads formed a rugby scrum and started pushing the OB back away from us. A load more lads joined in and a chant of, 'scrum, scrum, scrum' went up. It was funny as fuck. The coppers didn't know what to make of it. A couple of the coppers' helmets got knocked off during the commotion and one of them landed in our section of the crowd. It ended up getting thrown around the place, which kept us amused for a while.

The Old Bill eventually backed off a bit and we made our way to the train station, where our coach was waiting. We dropped the Wrexham lads off in Crewe so that they could get the train back home from there and dropped our younger lads off in Wigan so that they could go for a night on the piss. All things considered, we had managed to have a fairly good day out, despite the Old Bill's various attempts to piss us off.

'Violent clashes erupted in Nottingham city centre yesterday between police and members of the rightwing English Defence League,' writes Mark Townsend in *The Guardian*. 'Five hundred demonstrators from the EDL, many of whom had been drinking heavily, marched through Nottingham chanting: "We want our country back." . . . As night fell, hundreds of police officers escorted EDL protesters away from the city's main shopping streets in a security operation that was expected to cost about £1m.'

What *The Guardian* neglects to mention is that the Old Bill – whose massive operation cost more than £1 million – caused more trouble than they prevented. The BBC's website was equally biased in its reporting of the demo.

> Police have clashed with members of the English Defence League during a protest in Nottingham, with eleven people arrested. Some 300 demonstrators from the EDL marched through the city centre

shouting: 'We want our country back.' One of the 11 men arrested on suspicion of minor public order offences was also taken to hospital, with police saying it was believed he kicked a police dog, which then bit him.

It's funny how they twist these things around. The papers are always quick to point the finger at the EDL. They originally tried to accuse us of inciting racial hatred but now they have realised that there are many non-white members in our ranks, they have started saying that we are inciting religious hatred. That is an equally ridiculous claim for them to make, as we are not encouraging anybody to be hateful towards any other group. We only want to lay down some boundaries and prevent the Islamification of Britain. If this makes me either a racist or a bigot in the eyes of the public then so be it but I don't classify myself as either and I am going to carry on going to the rallies regardless of anybody else's views.

The EDL is Britain's last line of defence against the spread of Sharia law. Striking fear into the heart of anybody who opposes them with negative buzzwords like 'racist' and 'Islamophobic', the Islamic fundamentalists are trying to turn our streets into a breeding ground for extremists. I think the fact that rival football firms are willing to come together to register their support for our cause says a lot. I may be a hooligan but I care about this country and I am willing to speak out against those who wish to destroy the British way of life. I couldn't care less what Unite Against Fascism and groups with a similar ideology have to say. So long as Muslim extremists are preaching hate in our country, the EDL will continue to hold its demonstrations and the Bolton lads will carry on giving the organisation our full support. We aren't racist and we aren't anti-Islamic, we're merely pro-freedom and pro-democracy and nobody can find fault in that, no matter how hard they might try.

A few of the younger lads are pissed off with the EDL for allowing different ethnicities into the ranks. They're more into Combat 18 and the BNP and think that the organisation should have a whites-only policy. However, as with any group of our size, our members have a range of different opinions and political beliefs. I personally harbour no racial prejudice whatsoever but if lads want to hold those types of views then that's entirely up to them. So long as they are willing to stand and fight alongside the rest of us when something goes off then I really couldn't give a fuck. Graham is one of the racist members of our firm. Here is what he has got to say about Bolton's far right element...

Graham

I originally found out about the EDL from Kevin, who showed me a couple of videos of their marches on Facebook. I had always been interested in far-right politics and I was immediately drawn to them. One thing led to another and I ended up being the administrator of the Bolton EDL page.

To be honest with you, a lot of the lads that go to the EDL meetings have no political agenda whatsoever and most of them come along in the hope of being able to have a pop at another team's firm. Don't get me wrong, I'm bang into the British National Party and Combat 18 and all of that but that doesn't necessarily mean that the rest of the group share my opinions and, to be fair, Bolton is generally quite a racist place. The white parts of the town have been having regular battles with the Asian parts since I was a kid.

In The Haulgh where I'm from, one side is almost entirely white and the other half is almost entirely Asian. You can literally cross the street and go from a white area into an Asian one. They've got the advantage over us in a way though because there's always infighting amongst the white lads. We are a collection of independent factions, whereas they are able to come together as one.

Chris is the best person to fill you in on the various run-ins that we've had with the Asians. He's had a lot of trouble from them during his time with our firm but then again, he's given them an equal amount of grief in return.

Chris

Bolton is a very divided place and there has been a high degree of racial tension in the town from as far back as I can remember. The Asians tend to stay in Daubhill, Deane and Astley Bridge. There are none whatsoever in places like Tonge Moor and Little Lever and the only time we ever interact with them is when we're waging war against them.

One of our fiercest battles with the Asians happened as a result of somebody getting bottled by them while he was walking through the local park one night. Whenever something like that happens, there is always hell to pay and within a matter of minutes of hearing about the incident, we had gathered a small handful of our gamest lads together and were heading off into the night to look for them. Nobody can take liberties with our mates like that and expect to get away with it.

By the time we'd located our opponents, it was pitch black and we could hardly see a thing.

'Over there,' whispered one of our boys, pointing to a ten-strong mob of Pakistanis mooching about on this big hill at the top of Queen's Park. 'Let's get into them.'

The Asians managed to put up a valiant effort against us. One of them cracked me on the side of the head with an empty bottle of beer but I was able to pick the bottle up again just in time to smash another one of them repeatedly across the face with it before he got to me. I could feel the poor cunt's teeth cracking and snapping off as I belted him and after a good few minutes of hitting him, the cartilage in his nose eventually gave way. By the time I had finished with him, he looked like something out of a horror film. His head was gushing with blood and I must have beaten him half to death.

I was just about to ram the bottle into the bastard's face one last time when I heard an almighty roar and a load of Pakistanis came running down the hill towards us, armed with samurai swords and baseball bats. Now I'm not one to run away in a hurry but when your opponents are tooled up to fuck and you're completely unarmed, there really is no other option.

During the commotion, one of our lads lost his shoe in the mud and insisted on going back for it. He had just bought a pair of brand-new Reebok trainers and he was adamant that he was going to go home wearing them. Bad move. He ended up getting cut to fuck and he was left with big fuck-off slits along his arms and legs where the blade of a sword had sliced them. He gave as good as he got though. While he was getting chopped to pieces by the Asians, he managed to grab hold of a broken beer bottle and pushed it into one of his attackers' faces in a desperate attempt to get them off him. The lad on the receiving end went away with a big, round slash mark where the glass had entered his flesh.

The kid who got chopped up with the sword ended up with a total of a hundred stitches. That's the Asians for you though. I'll give them credit where it's due: they are always able to pull together a sizeable mob at a moment's *notice but they rely too heavily upon weapons. It is very rare that you'll end up getting a fair fight with them. They are the ultimate tool merchants and a lot of them can't actually have a scrap. They think that they're as hard as nails when they're sneaking up on you from behind and hitting you with a bat but when it comes to knuckling up, they're a bunch of fucking cowards.*

At this point, you're probably thinking, 'How can you claim that you aren't a racist firm when your younger lads are having regular race wars with the Asians?' Well just because some of our members are racist, it doesn't mean that racism is part of our firm's policy. Besides, I'd say that it was more of a disagreement between two different sets of people rather than a racially motivated attack. Don't get me wrong, Chris is a self-confessed racist but this particular incident was just a case of him and his mates retaliating against somebody who had attacked one of their friends.

The Asians aren't the only ethnic group to feel the wrath of the Bolton Youth firm over the last few years. There are a lot of Kosovans in Bolton and they get just as much aggro, even though they're white. Our racist element doesn't like anybody who isn't from the same neck of the woods, no matter what ethnicity they are. They'll fight with anybody, irrespective of their colour, creed or nationality. According to Kevin, the main reason that our youth firm get into so many fights with the Kosovans is because they're always up for a scrap . . .

Kevin

The fights with the Kosovans have been some of the best we've had. They're game as fuck, the lot of them. You only have to glance in their direction and they'll be calling their mates up, trying to get a little mob together. I remember when we were stood behind this Kosovan fella in Bolton town centre and he kept on swearing so my mate went over to him and told him to calm himself down.

'Fuck you,' the fella snarled at him. 'Go and fuck yourself.'

'Woah, woah, woah,' I told the Kosovan. 'Don't you speak to him like that.'

I was trying to wind him up, making out that I was keen to keep the peace but at the same time secretly hoping for it to go off.

'Fuck yourself,' the Kosovan yelled. 'I got knife. I cut you.'

The minute he mentioned that he had a blade my mate jumped in and whacked him in the face. It is best not to risk waiting around to gauge whether or not somebody's bluffing when they're on about pulling tools out.

The Kosovans are similar to the Asians in that they can pull a decent-sized mob together in no time at all and, within a matter of minutes, the streets were crawling with the fuckers. They managed to hold their own against us but we eventually came out on top and the fella that had claimed to have the knife ended up lying on the floor, getting kicked to fuck. Several of his mates got the same treatment, which has hopefully taught them to show a little more respect. I wouldn't travel across to Kosovo and randomly kick off with a load of their lot so what gives them the right to do it over here? They got what they deserved and if that makes me a racist then I'm a fucking racist.

So there you have it. Kevin and his mates didn't go out targeting innocent Kosovan refugees: they were provoked into a fight by a fella claiming to have a knife on him. We're portrayed as being a bunch of racist thugs but, in reality, we've had a lot more fights with our white British rivals than we've had with blacks, Kosovans or Asians. Sure we've got a couple of genuine racists within our ranks but then again, who hasn't?

8
THE YOUTH

Now that you've heard all about the battles that our older firm have had, both against rival football firms and against the political correctness brigade as part of the EDL, it's time for me to fill you in on what the younger generation have been up to. Graham has agreed to give you an account of his time with the Bolton Youth mob on condition that his version of events is left completely unedited. Here's what he's got to say . . .

Graham

The first game I ever attended was in 1994, making me nine years old at the time. It was a first-division fixture between Bolton and Notts County at Burnden Park. I had finally, after months of pestering, managed to persuade my father to take me, even though he detested football and everything to do with it. I can remember queuing to get into the ground and asking my dad all sorts of questions that had nothing to do with the match. All of my questions were about the away fans. 'How many will they bring?' and 'Can we sit near the Notts County fans and give them stick?'

Now to this day I can't remember the score, what the game was like or in fact any detail whatsoever about what happened on the pitch because for the whole game, I was watching the small pocket of away fans stood on the terraces next to the Burnden Paddock. I found it all fascinating: the banter, the singing, the chanting, the general hostility shown to the other side. Unlike other boys my age, I wasn't interested in the football. I was far more interested in studying the behaviour on that side of the ground.

The reason I've chose to start with this memory from my first football match is because I think it gives a good insight into the question that is asked of so many football hooligans. Why? Why do we do what we do? What possesses us to run around on a Saturday afternoon causing mayhem, fighting other groups of hooligans and putting our safety at risk and our freedom in jeopardy? I believe that football violence is something that is in you. You've either got it in you or you haven't. Many psychologists would love to tell you that there are social reasons behind why many young men get involved. They say that we are men from broken homes or with abusive fathers or deprived childhoods. In some cases that may be true but all those men will tell you that they were born with it in them. I always knew from the first match I went to that I would eventually become involved in the darker side of football. It was only a matter of time. Was I from a broken home and did I have a deprived childhood? No, far from it. My parents were both university educated, both professional and we were well off.

I don't believe that you can wake up one day and suddenly decide, 'Right, I'm gonna be a football hooligan.' There has got to be something in your brain that draws you to it, like a moth to light, and once you've had a taste it is more addictive than drugs or drink. Friends of mine have often said to me, 'You're an idiot. Why look for trouble? You could get seriously hurt.' Every lad knows the risks before he goes into battle but for those of us with this indescribable attraction to hooliganism we just can't stay away. It's like a magnetic field drawing us in. So whenever anybody asks me why I do what I do I always reply with the same answer: 'I can't explain it in any way you'd even begin to understand.' If you've ever taken part in football violence, you'll know exactly what we mean. If you haven't then you'll think that we're a load of fucking morons!

Here is an account of my first ever battle alongside Bolton's youth firm . . .

I received a text from an older Bolton lad about a week before this trip telling me that some of the Halliwell youth lads had been battling with Bradford in Manchester some weeks before and that this had been organised as a revenge mission. Halliwell's top youth lad had been in touch with Bradford by phone to make all the arrangements for a meet. I had spent most of my time travelling to games with the older element of our mob and I didn't really know any of the youth lads but I thought, 'fuck it, if something's planned then I'm game'.

I arrived at the Sharman Arms pub on Halliwell Road at about ten. It was a Saturday game and there were a good twenty to twenty-five lads there already, drinking and taking drugs, ready for the day ahead. Two minibuses had been ordered and I was told by Kevin – the lad who ran the mob – that we were going to join forces with Rochdale's youth for the day to fight Bradford.

In the end we numbered approximately thirty to thirty-five lads, ages ranging from seventeen to twenty-three. It was a good turnout considering we were going to someone else's fixture. I know some mobs who can't even pull that for their home games. Some of the lads in the pub were from Great Lever, Little Lever and Astley Bridge but the core of the youth mob were from Halliwell and had grown up together.

We'd arranged to meet Rochdale's lads in a pub on Whitworth Road called the Brickmaker's Arms, which was a short distance from Rochdale town centre. We arrived at the boozer and piled out and I thought that we had a good, solid mob that would take some budging. We filed into the pub one by one and Rochdale's little outfit were there waiting for us. They looked a lot younger, smaller and scruffier than us. One of their lads had a pair of mud-stained Reebok Classics on and I thought 'fucking hell, I had a pair of them when I was twelve'. But then again, he probably was twelve! At twenty-three years of age, I was suddenly starting to feel old.

The only two lads of any note stature-wise were their main lad and a fat kid with a black coat on. Them two looked the part but, as for the rest of them, they were a joke and we all knew it. We had turned more lads out for their game than them. I would say they turned out a scruffy twenty at best.

We stayed in the Brickmaker's, planning what we were going to do and taking advice from the Rochdale lads about getting away from the police if it went tits up because they obviously knew their manor better than us. We were playing pool and having a few drinks when Kevin came over and told a few of us that if it didn't go off with Bradford then we'd just twat Rochdale so as not to have a wasted trip. We started laughing and agreed and soon word got round to everyone what the plan was if things didn't go the way we wanted them to go. We were there for Bradford but if that didn't happen we would be guaranteed to get it because we would just destroy Rochdale's pathetic mob.

Luckily for them, we got enough action out of Bradford to save them a hiding.

After about an hour, the police were all over the place and they had put riot vans and officers the length of Whitworth Road. We knew that Bradford's mob must have arrived somewhere on the scene and so everybody started to get animated. The Rochdale lads started singing one of their songs and we belted out our great Bolton Youth battle cry: 'We're Bolton, we're white, we're here to fucking fight. Where's your boys? Where's your boys?'

In the middle of all the noise, one of the lads got a bit too excited and decided to punch a window through at the front of the pub. We decided to exit through the back gate of the beer garden but discovered that it was locked on police orders. The main Rochdale lad persuaded the barman to unlock it and let us leave, which didn't take much as his premises were being vandalised by the lads inside.

We made a swift exit, ran down the back streets behind the Brickmaker's and remained unnoticed by the police, who were still lining Whitworth Road. There was a crossroad in front of us with a car dealership on the right-hand side and two tall, mill-like buildings on either side. Bradford's mob turned the corner at the bottom of the street and started to walk up between the two large buildings. They had also been drinking on Whitworth Road at a pub further down called the Tanner's Arms. They came round the corner in groups of around twenty until they filled the whole street. I'd say at a rough estimate that they numbered 150–200 and these lads weren't kids. It was a pretty awesome sight and I'd not seen a mob of that size and calibre before. This was a proper mob, organised and experienced. However, we were as game as any of the lads in their mob. We were young and heavily outnumbered but we gave it everything we had.

As their mob came up the road, a few of us went forward and stood our ground at the crossroad and waited for the Bradford hordes to come onto us. I looked behind me and our mob was scattered up the road. Obviously a lot of people had seen their arses. Rochdale's young pretenders in particular had slowed down until they were nearly at a snail's pace and, all of a sudden, the excitement they displayed at the pub had drained away. They were more interested in standing at the back and filming everything on their mobile phones than they were in fighting.

I glanced in both directions and I saw Kevin on one side and a lad called

Harry on the other, so I knew I was in good company. Another lad called Bobbie had advanced ten yards or so further on into the street that Bradford were coming down and, at one point, I thought that he was going to steam into them on his own but he soon retreated after being hit by some friendly fire. A bottle thrown by one of our lot had clocked him on the head.

At this point, the police were still scratching their arses on Whitworth Road, leaving both mobs to go at it. Bradford got about twenty yards from us and then steamed in. The six or seven of us that were at the front took the full brunt and we were soon swallowed up by their superior numbers. We took a few blows but we gave as good as we got. Kevin had a tooth knocked out and Bobbie took a bit of a beating. I took a good crack on the cheek after missing with a big haymaker of my own. The rest of our lads were now behind us as back up but we just couldn't cope with Bradford's numbers. We traded blows with them toe to toe for what was probably only about twenty seconds but seemed like an eternity.

The police soon got wind of what was going on, as the huge roar from the crossroads was echoing down the street between the two buildings and the noise of the battle was deafening. We scattered as they came in, batoning anything that moved and then we fucked off in the direction we had come from. Bradford were herded back down the street that they had come from as well.

We all agreed afterwards that if it wasn't for the police intervention, we'd have got a good hiding because we definitely weren't expecting to run into such a monster. We were supposed to be settling a score with the Bradford youth but we ended up tackling their entire mob. We were few but we were brave.

Bradford were soon ballooning that they had done Bolton's main mob but I would like to point out to them that I was the oldest lad on that crossroads at the age of twenty-three. I would like to think that some respect was forthcoming from them after the fight we put up. I can still safely say that Bradford's mob that day was the best mob I have ever seen and we were lucky to get away with just a few cuts and bruises.

We were soon rounded up by the police, although some lads got away and stayed in Rochdale. They tried to arrange something with just Bradford's youth but it didn't materialise.

As they had us up against the wall, taking our details, one of the coppers asked, 'Are you lot fucking stupid? Have you seen how many of them there are?' and I replied, 'Yeah, I know mate, we've just fucking seen them.' At that point,

THE YOUTH

I put my hand up to rub the lump that was slowly starting to emerge on my cheek. We were then fucked off back to Bolton and told not to come back.

We learned a few valuable lessons that day. Firstly, we learnt not to underestimate any mob because Bradford had certainly given us a surprise. Secondly, we learnt that Rochdale has the worst and the scruffiest youth mob in the country and, thirdly, we learnt what it was like to be together and up against it. I know it sounds gay but we bonded and cemented the trust and the friendship between us. Even in the stickiest of situations, we had the character and bottle to pull through.

This day was the birth of Bolton's youth mob and it was the catalyst for us becoming one of the most active mobs in the country, not just in youth terms but out of all mobs. We went from being young, game lads to a hardcore, ruthless group of individuals with a dangerous, uncompromising attitude. We weren't concerned with cameras or banning orders or jail sentences. We were interested in one thing only and that was fighting anyone and everyone, any time, any place. And that hardcore of lads is still there today. The fact that we are all on banning orders hasn't stopped our appetite for football violence. It has just made us plan better, prepare more and go to even greater lengths to feed our addiction to violence. No town is off limits, no game is too big for us to turn up unannounced and cause mayhem. We've done it so many times in the past and no doubt we will do it well into the future.

Here's what Kevin, Bolton Youth's top lad, has got to say about their firm . . .

Kevin

Before I got into the whole football-violence thing, I was involved in fighting with gangs from different parts of Bolton. I grew up in Halliwell, which is one of the roughest areas in the town, and we were constantly at war with Astley Bridge.

When I was twelve or thirteen, I started hearing stories about what the football lads had been up to and I can remember wanting to be like them. It was like the next step up from having it out with Astley Bridge. Rather than different areas within Bolton fighting one another, it was entire towns rowing with one another. I was drawn to it from the first time I heard about it and, by the time I was fifteen, I'd got a little group of mates together and we were saving all our money to travel to the away games.

At first, the older lads just saw us as a load of little nuggets. We were young and inexperienced and nobody really rated us. The turning point came during a game against Notts Forest when five of us ganged up on these two fully grown men and we managed to get them to the floor and leather them. We ended up kicking them to fuck and from then on the more established hooligans started seeing us in a different light. It was the first time I'd been in the thick of things and I was buzzing about it for weeks to come.

As the years went by, our group of mates developed into a proper little firm and we started recruiting people from different areas of the town to travel to the matches. None of us were exactly the hardest lads in the world but we were all proper game and we were never ones to shy away from a fight.

As far as Bolton's main firm were concerned, we were still a bunch of nobodies. They were unwilling to give us the time of day because of our age and we were hell-bent on turning their opinion of us around.

'There's only one thing for it,' I told the rest of our lads. 'We're going to have to do something stupid to make a name for ourselves. At our game against Blackburn this weekend, let's all go in their seats.'

Going into other people's ends was regarded as something that had died out by the end of the 1990s. Nobody had done it for ages and we wanted to be known as the firm that dared to go where others feared to tread. It would show that we meant business and, with a bit of luck, we would finally gain the respect of the entire firm.

Sure enough, twenty Bolton Youth bought tickets for Blackburn's end and as soon as it got to half-time, we put a Bolton Wanderers flag up across the walkway at the front of their seats. Almost the second the flag was up, a huge horde of Blackburn lads came running across the stand, looking to beat the fuck out of us. Cans of drink were raining down on us right, left and centre and even the women and children were going mad, calling us every name under the sun.

Blackburn's mob ended up running down the steps to have it with us and we were scrapping with them for a good couple of minutes before the coppers showed up. A fair few of us got banned that day but we had achieved our goal. Our invasion of their end was the talk of the town for weeks to come and after that we started to get a bit more recognition off the older lads. We were no longer seen as a bunch of teenage tagalongs, we were now officially part of Bolton's firm.

I got a three-year ban for my part in the disruption. There was no proper closed-circuit television at Blackburn's ground in those days but they had official match photographers stationed around the pitch and one of them had managed to take a picture of me and another lad going at it.

The sanctions placed on me meant nothing, because I had always found the 'violence' part of 'football violence' to be far more appealing than the 'football' part. Although I was banned from every ground in the country, there was nothing that they could do to stop me arranging fights away from the games. They may have prevented me from kicking off at the matches but my love of hooliganism had only just begun. From that day on, I have been scrapping with rival mobs up and down the country at every available opportunity.

The coppers think they're smart with all their cameras and football-intelligence officers and all that shit but, at the end of the day, if you arrange your battles beforehand on the phone and properly plan them out then there's no way they can stop you. Fair enough they've made it harder to kick off outside the grounds but that's it really. They have shifted the problem away from the matches but football violence will always exist in one form or another and whatever they do to stop us, we'll always find a way to carry on doing what we do.

The day that we successfully invaded Blackburn's end was one of the few times that we've actually been able to get them to have a scrap with us. They're one of the worst mobs in the country and it's almost impossible to get a fight round those parts. Saying that, we had a decent run-in with Man City's firm in the neighbouring town of Darwen a couple of months ago. We had arranged to meet up with the City mob round there so that the Old Bill wouldn't get onto us and one of our lads had gone into their pub, dressed in trackies so that they wouldn't know he was a hooligan.

Wigan were playing Blackburn later on that day and some Wigan lads had decided to team up with City. There were twenty-five City lads on one side of the boozer and ten to fifteen Wigan on the other and they were busy discussing how they were supposedly going to do us, completely oblivious to the fact that they had a spy in their midst. It was time for us to make our presence known.

When we first walked into the pub, we didn't even know that City were in there. We had gone into the side that the Wigan supporters were in and *assumed that they were the only ones about. One of them picked up a glass and threw it at one of our lads so I grabbed him by his hair, dragged him out of the door and twatted him. The rest of Bolton Youth were quick to follow my example and, within a matter of minutes, we had successfully leathered Wigan's entire mob. Now it was time to do the same to City.*

City were gathered round the pool tables and the minute we drew near to them, they started chucking pool balls at us and picking up the cues, ready to smack us with them. Nobody wanted to be the first one into the fray but I eventually led the way and was immediately whacked around the face with a pool cue. Luckily, the lad that hit me with it had decided to smack me with the thin end, which wasn't capable of doing too much damage. The minute the cue made contact, I grabbed it off him, turned it around and split his forehead wide open with it.

While all this was going on, one of my mates was busy hammering a bar stool into another lad's head. It was a pretty hefty stool and I had to stop him from hitting the City lad with it in the end because it was looking likely that he was going to end up killing him.

Within five minutes of it going off, ten of City's firm were laying on the floor, bleeding like fuck and wishing they had stayed at home. The inside of the boozer was a total mess. The windows were smashed, there was broken glass all over the floor and the pool table had been emptied of its contents. A terrified Man City lad attempted to clamber through the broken window to safety but he was grabbed around the waist and thrown across the floor. Part of his thumb was missing from where he'd sliced it open on a jagged shard of glass and he was leaking pools of claret all over the place.

One of the Mancs was lying on the floor crying his eyes out while all this was going on. He had been given a right good hiding and looked as if he had been in a car crash. The rest of their firm eventually ended up climbing through a window and running away to safety, which was annoying because I wanted to carry on twatting them. We had just left the pub to look for them when a load of Old Bill turned up, causing everybody to scatter. Seven lads ended up getting nicked but it was a small price to pay. I'd had the time of my life and I would have gladly taken a night in the cells in return for a fight like that.

Here's what Graham's got to say about what went on in Darwen that day. Once again, his account has been left exactly as he wrote it . . .

THE YOUTH

Graham

This fixture came hot on the heels of the Bradford versus Rochdale game and there was still a certain level of hype and hysteria surrounding the events that had taken place that day. Word about what went down had circulated round the youth groups in Bolton, resulting in an over-inflated turnout for us against City. It was as if everyone had heard free money was being handed out and they all wanted a piece of the action.

In the days leading up to the game, everybody was buzzing in anticipation of more fun and games. City had been spoken to and we had arranged for everything to go off in West Houghton, a small town that is part of the Bolton borough and lies between Bolton town centre and Horwich, Horwich being where the Reebok stadium is situated. This was ideal for us, as it wasn't far for us to travel from our usual meeting point at the Sharman Arms on Halliwell Road.

Around thirty of us met up at 10.30 on Saturday morning. We had a few quick pints and then got minibuses to the Howfener pub on Bolton Road in West Houghton. Chris had squared everything up with a barman the night before and arranged it so that we could stay undetected and well out of sight without having to worry about the police turning up or the staff ringing the authorities. We always planned out what we were going to do well in advance to give ourselves the best chance of having it off. Half of the battle is keeping yourselves low key and off the Old Bill's radar, which we did by popping in to see the barman of the boozer the night before the meet to butter him up and assure him that a load of lads would be putting money behind his bar and causing no problems. In return, he had to guarantee not to give our cover away to the police or start flapping and giving in to them if they did turn up for whatever reason. Sometimes we would manage to get ourselves into enemy territory without being detected only for the landlord of the first boozer we walked into to spoil it for us by getting straight on the blower to the coppers. Some of these incidents will be mentioned later in this chapter.

Having got nice and settled in the Howfener, I noticed that a group of lads had turned up that I'd never seen before and was told by the Halliwell lads that they were lads from around the Chorley Old Road area of Bolton. They had decided to come along even though they famously didn't get on with the Halliwell lads, as they had been drawn in by the tales of what had gone on during the previous weeks. Kevin had invited them a few nights beforehand and an uneasy truce seemed to have been struck. They boosted our numbers to a good forty lads.

After around forty-five minutes of drinking and sniffing, everybody was eager to know where City were, as the plan was to have it early and get off back to Halliwell to have a day on the piss. Kevin received a phone call from the City lads and they dropped the bombshell that they weren't going to be meeting us after all because they had opted to travel to Oldham to give them a hand, as they were at home to Millwall that day. A lot of the lads were disappointed, especially the ones who were turning out for the first time, but to the rest of us this was just a minor setback. Some questioned City's motives for refusing to come to where their side was playing but I reasoned that, given the chance, most of us would rather have a crack at Millwall than City so it worked both ways.

We immediately got the paper out to seek out an alternative fixture to attend, as there was no point hanging around for City when we knew that they were going to Oldham. We didn't want to call it a day at 1 p.m. with forty lads out eager to cause mayhem and luckily the disappointment didn't last long, as Blackburn were at home to Wigan. This was going to be a naughty day. The minibuses were immediately ordered and we set off to Darwen, which is just on the other side of the moors, between Bolton and Blackburn, and about two to three miles away from Blackburn's ground. This is where every away side's fans at Blackburn go drinking before and after the game.

We arrived in Darwen at about 1.45 and went into the White Lion, which is a big pub on a hill overlooking the town centre. The landlady was nice and friendly and as I've already said, Darwen is the location that all of the away fans drink in on match days. This means that the landlords of the pubs in Darwen are used to seeing big groups of football lads so we knew it wouldn't come on top with the police.

The next three hours were very uneventful. They were bordering on boring to be honest. It was very quiet and the prospect of it going off seemed extremely remote. A few lads who had driven down in their cars got off and reduced our numbers to between thirty and thirty-five. Kevin wasn't worried, as it was still a tasty mob and we had not only the Wigan lads to wait for coming back into Darwen from the game but also the Darwen-based Blackburn lads, that is if they actually exist because I've been to Blackburn watching Bolton numerous times and never seen them. Blackburn's mob is like Keyser Söze in the movie 'The Usual Suspects'. It's just some spook story and no-one has ever seen him.

At quarter to five we had our first sniff of a lad, when five unwitting older Wigan heads walked into the White Lion. As soon as they saw us, they knew that they were in trouble. We were like a pack of hyenas, sniffing around our prey ready to attack. But we didn't just want to do five sad old men. We wanted a proper brawl so Kevin asked them where the rest of their lads were. They tried to claim that they weren't lads and were just normos having a pint after the match. This didn't wash with Kevin, as one of them had a big Stone Island coat on. Now it's well known in football hooligan circles that you don't wear Stone Island unless you're a lad. Kevin said to him, 'Listen, you don't wear Stone Island unless you're after it so where's all your lads?' At this point they still thought we were Blackburn but then the colour ran from their faces as we told them that we were Bolton. A big, burly cunt – who was about six foot five and forty years old – just turned and walked out of the pub, saying 'I don't need this, I'm too old.'

Wigan and Bolton have a long and deep-running rivalry so these lads knew the worst position that they could find themselves in was in a pub full of Bolton. The remaining four lads also made for the exit and we let them go, as we hadn't come all this way to do four or five blokes. We had come to have it off proper. If they had walked in with fifteen to twenty of them then it would have been a different matter and we would have pasted them. The thing about our youth mob is that we'll always go in search of other teams' older lots and have it with them rather than going for their youth. That's not because we're arrogant or think we're better than anyone else but because we want a good fight. If we come out on the losing side then so be it but no-one can say we bottle it. We always put ourselves about, no matter the numbers.

The landlady soon rang the police and pointed Kevin out, telling them that he was goading the Wigan lads to fight, which was pretty accurate. Luckily there were no arrests and we were allowed on our way. We walked down the hill to the next pub along, which was a big fuck-off one on the corner called the Millstone. It didn't take long for a few more likely figures to walk in and the atmosphere was on a knife-edge once more. This time they were local lads and seemed pissed off that we had wolf-whistled and directed the term 'sweetheart' towards them to try and entice them into fighting us.

After a quick scan of the pub, they soon learned of our numbers and sank into their shells, cowering by the bar. Once again, Kevin engaged them in conversation to try and find out where Blackburn's lads were and if they fancied it. The local lads reply confirmed what we had known for years.

'Blackburn haven't got any lads,' they said. 'You're best off looking for Wigan.'

Ten minutes later, we got a phone call from City saying that they were on their way to Darwen with about twenty to twenty-five lads. All of a sudden things were looking up. Kevin had been updating City all day long about our whereabouts and they had finally agreed to come and have it. Darwen was the ideal location. There were very few cameras and police around, as they were all at the ground and on the Blackburn side of town.

City soon landed and told us that they were in a pub called the Railway, which was a short walk from the Millstone. We sent a couple of lads up to see if they were indeed there. As soon as they rang with the confirmation, we were going to set off and smash them.

The phone call came and we set off walking up a steep slope leading to the pub, which was bang opposite Darwen railway station but well out the way of the town-centre cameras. We slowly entered the pub in dribs and drabs and there were only fifteen to twenty of us in there to begin with. The boozer had a strange layout because there were two sides to the bar but only one way in and out of the pub so the poolroom was shut off from the main vault. The City lads were in the poolroom, unaware of our presence. There were around six lads in the main bar and there came a moment just before it was about to kick off when nobody was quite sure who was who.

'We're Bolton. Are we having it or what?' Chris belted out to break the silence.

At that, all hell broke loose. The six lads in the pub were Wigan and one of them emptied his glass and hurled it towards us. Chris caught it in one hand and threw it back with the other and we all steamed into them. There was a human blockade at the door as fists and boots went flying. Everyone was trying to get out of the door at the same time, which resulted in a jam.

The daft Wigan cunt who had thrown the pint glass was dragged out of the pub by his hair and dealt with. We steamed out of the pub and continued to give the Wigan lads a good hiding until they got on their toes and hurried away to the station. One of them was bleeding heavily as a result of a stool over the head.

Everybody began to walk away, thinking 'job well done'. Then P pointed out that City were still in the poolroom on the other side. We roared back into the pub, half tripping over the broken furniture that lay strewn in the doorway. The City lads knew what was coming, as they had seen the events unfolding through the window, and one of their lads made a feeble attempt to meet us head on in the passageway between the main room of the pub and the poolroom. He was met with a pint glass to the head and then a volley of uppercuts, as one of our lads gripped him by the scruff of the neck and proceeded to beat him back to where he came from.

We reached the doorway and poured in like ants. City were like rabbits in the headlights. They didn't know what to do. They only numbered around twelve to fifteen lads. They had walked into a monster and they knew it. You could smell the fear in the room. As we came through the doorway, a few bottles and chairs were half-heartedly thrown at us but nothing was going to stop the onslaught that ensued. The pool balls and cues that had started in their hands were now in ours and rained down on them with no mercy. The first four or five City lads were absolutely demolished. Blood was everywhere. It was on the floor and on the walls.

The rest of their lads retreated to the back of the room and such was the severity of our attack that they had to break the window at the front of the pub to escape. Two of their lads battered the window with a stool until it broke and scrambled through to escape the terror that continued inside the room. In their haste to get away, one of the City lads sliced his thumb off whilst clambering through the broken window. Everyone was now in the room and we wanted a piece of the action. The City lads were so bowled over by the sheer ferocity and momentum of our attack that they didn't have an answer. They all managed to escape apart from one poor cunt who had blood pissing down his face and was trembling with fright. The only words he could utter were, 'I'm sorry. I'm sorry.' The response from us was uncompromising. It was 'You shouldn't be fucking around organising fights with us then,' followed by a stool over the head causing him to drop to the ground. We fucked off straight away, scaling the back fence of the pub and getting off down the street. All of a sudden, about ten lads emerged at the top of the street, calling it on. We bounced towards them thinking it was City but it turned out to be some of our lads who had been at the front of the pub, getting into the City lads as they escaped through the window.

We didn't just hand a hiding out to City, it was an absolute pasting. They walked into a monster and I guarantee it's a day they will never forget. Why they turned up with twelve to fifteen lads is beyond me because we made no secret of our numbers. I can only think that they were either arrogant or stupid, or maybe both. One of our lads asked me if I respected them for still turning up with that many lads and I said 'no'. Why? Because it wasn't brave, it was just plain stupid. Did they seriously think that they were going to do thirty-five of us with only fifteen of them there? Yes, it has been done before, but we ain't no fucking mugs. We had a top mob out that day and they knew it but yet they still came with those numbers. To me, that is disrespectful because they brought us out in numbers expecting a good fight with their full mob and then turned up six hours late after fucking us off for Oldham versus Millwall with a scruffy fifteen lads. They got what they deserved and I can safely say they won't take anybody as lightly as they took us that day again because that annihilation will live long in the memory of those lads and will hurt for a long, long time.

The sound of sirens soon filled the air. At this point it was every man for himself so we split up to try and avoid being nicked. Unfortunately, a number of lads from both sides, including myself, were arrested near the scene and held for twenty-four hours. Luckily for us, the CCTV in the pub was shocking and no further action was brought against anyone. It was a lucky escape for all involved, as a lot of people would have been doing a lot of jail time if it had been better.

This started what has become a long-running feud between us and City, with them clearly after revenge for what took place in Darwen. We've now had three to four battles with City, all of which have been pre-arranged with more or less even numbers, and they are yet to do us. That's because we don't take anyone lightly and for some reason City just can't get one over on us, despite having one of the best up-and-coming mobs, along with ourselves.

Nowadays I would say that Bolton's youth are easily on a par with the older firm. They are one of the most active mobs in the country and they've taken some formidable opponents on throughout the years. Kevin is as game a lad as you're ever likely to meet and he's a natural born leader. The youth firm are the future of the Cuckoo Boys and I would say that the future is definitely looking bright.

9
THE WALKDEN WHITES

While young Kevin enjoys the violence more than the football, I'd say that they go hand in hand for me. I am a football hooligan but I am also a football supporter and I don't always go to the matches looking for a fight. When I want to have a row, I go with the Cuckoo Boys but when I want to watch the game and have a bit of a laugh, I go with a group of loyal Bolton fans known as the Walkden Whites. They are not hooligans and they don't cause trouble, although they do like to have a drink and they can get boisterous at times.

The Walkden Whites is a supporters club with well over a hundred members, ranging from kids in prams to old men in their sixties. It's a very family-orientated group and there are a lot of women and children involved. I have always kept my violent side under control whenever I have gone to the matches with them, although there was one occasion on which I had some random lunatic threatening me for no apparent reason and had no choice but to react.

It started off like any other away game. We met outside the Stocks pub in Walkden with a carrier bag full of tinnies and parked ourselves on a picnic bench at six o'clock in the morning, waiting for our coach. As I've said before, the Whites like their drink. They don't get violent when they're drunk but they really do like a piss up. We were heading off to Tottenham, which is a good four hours drive away from Bolton, and by the time we had arrived at the ground, we were all proper bladdered.

We were drinking all through the game and on our way home we decided to stop off in Rugby so that we could get a couple more pints in. There was a wedding reception taking place at our stop-off point and the bride and groom were a right mismatch. This weird-looking ginger bloke had married a short, fat Asian bird and they didn't seem particularly happy to see us.

'I know your type,' the newly married bride leered across the pub at us. 'You're a bunch of bloody hoogilans.'

Eh? I'd heard of a hooligan before but I'd never heard of a 'hoogilan'.

'That's right,' she told us, 'You're a load of fucking hoogilans, the lot of you.'

'Look,' I told her, 'We don't want any trouble and we haven't come to disrupt your do. We'll stay on this side of the pub away from your reception and that way we won't cramp your style.'

The tubby Asian munter was having none of it.

'You better make sure you do stay away from us,' she snarled. 'I don't like hoogilans and I don't want them around me.'

I was tempted to ask her what the fuck a hoogilan was but I decided to keep my mouth shut in the hope that she'd fuck off.

A couple of minutes later, Mickey, one of our lads, came furtively sneaking out of the toilets, alongside a certain overweight Pakistani bird.

'You'll never guess what I've just done,' he told me, grinning from ear to ear as he spoke. 'I've just got a blowjob off that bloke's new missus.'

It was funny as fuck but I couldn't help feeling sorry for the groom. He had only just got married and his wife had already had another man's cock in her mouth.

Sure enough, half an hour down the line, the ginger fella came stomping across the pub to confront us. I don't know whether he had heard about the blowjob or whether he was just annoyed that we were still in the pub. Either way he was determined to cause a scene.

'I've heard that you've been giving my wife a hard time,' he told me. 'We don't need hooligans in here. We've only just got married. What's your fucking problem?'

'She's my fucking problem,' I told him. 'She keeps on calling me a hoogilan. Can you two please just fuck off and leave me alone? I won't bother you if you don't bother me.'

It was like trying to reason with a lump of stone. He obviously wanted a fight and I was rapidly losing my temper.

'Leave my wife alone, you hear me?' he ranted. 'She doesn't like hooligans, neither of us do.'

He was getting in my face and shouting and screaming at me so I gave him a single tap to the jaw and knocked the mouthy cunt straight out. His dad came flying across the pub to have it with me so I chinned him and knocked him out as well.

'Come on,' said Jimmy, one of the Walkden lot. 'We need to make a move before the situation gets any worse.'

I really didn't want to hit the fella. It was bad enough that Mickey had been ramming his knob down his ugly wife's throat on the day that they'd got married. I'm not the type of person who will go around randomly ruining a couple's wedding receptions but, at the end of the day, if somebody is hassling you non-stop for no particular reason then you are going to get annoyed. It was completely unavoidable and he brought it on himself. It was one of the few occasions in which an outing with the Whites was marred by violence and it was a shame that it had to happen.

Peaceful as they are, the Whites have had their fair share of arrests over the years. The Bolton Old Bill have given out bans to several of their members and told the rest of the group that they're going to end up getting arrested if they don't do what they're told. The authorities have attempted to brand the Walkden lot as hooligans because they like to have a drink but that couldn't be further from the truth. They have a laugh and can be loud at times but they are all pacifists and have never instigated a fight in all the time I've known them.

Here's Frank Haslam, the founding member of the Whites, to tell you about the various run-ins that he's had with the coppers, despite the fact that he's probably never broken a law in his life . . .

Frank

We're undoubtedly one of the most nonconformist supporters clubs in the country. We don't conform to anything that the police tell us to do because we don't see why we should be herded into the ground and made to do what they say.

None of our members are violent in any way whatsoever. They just want to have a good time so why should they be made to follow the police's instructions? The authorities are constantly trying to tell us when and where we can meet up but we don't want to be strictly regimented. We're human beings, not sheep, and we can make our own decisions without the need for official police guidelines.

Certain police officers have made no bones about the fact that they're out to get us. They tell us, 'We'll get you. You must conform or we'll get you.' They couldn't make it any clearer if they tried but, at the end of the day, we control our own members and we're completely self-policing. If any of our guys step out of line, we are fully capable of dealing with them ourselves without the need for anybody else getting involved. Most of the bans that the police have issued us with have been imposed for manufactured reasons and we've been unfairly persecuted for our unwillingness to have our actions dictated to us by the powers that be.

Some of our members have been banned for completely fabricated reasons, never mind manufactured ones. 'Five Bolton Wanderers fans received banning orders for their behaviour at Anfield on Boxing Day' wrote a reporter for the *Liverpool Echo* on 16 January 2009. What they failed to mention was that one of them was arrested for making a supposedly racist remark during a private conversation and another, Colin Hamblett, was basically banned for nothing. He was a little bit tipsy but that was it.

The coppers have even previously admitted that Colin has never laid a finger on anyone, describing him in their intelligence file as, 'Always raucous, always drunk, never violent.' If banning people from grounds was a measure brought in to prevent football hooliganism then how do they justify imposing it on someone that they've admitted is completely non-violent? It seems illogical to me.

While it is true that he has never intentionally started a fight at a football match, that's not to say Colin hasn't been kicked off on. Whereas the vast majority of hooligans are deeply opposed to attacking your average, shirt-wearing supporter, there is a handful who will target anybody that ventures into their town. Shrewsbury's English Border Front are one such firm and they proved what a bunch of bullying bastards they are when they randomly laid into the Walkden Whites while they were at an away game. Here's Colin to tell you how he got his revenge on a set of hooligans with no sense of morality whatsoever, demonstrating that the only time he would ever resort to violence was when he was responding in kind.

Colin

I'm not the type of fella who goes to football matches to have a fight. I've got nothing against the people who do but I go there to get pissed up and to have a laugh. Saying that though, I am not exactly one to follow orders either and when the landlady of the pub that we were in told me not to go into the pool room, I couldn't resist going in.

'Scotty's in there,' she told me. 'He's the leader of Shrewsbury's firm.'

At the time I hadn't even heard of their mob and I really didn't think that I had too much to worry about. After all, we were just your average, run-of-the-mill supporters. We hadn't come for any bother so why would anybody want to give us any?

We were just settling down to play a game of pool when an angry-looking football lad came storming into the room, looking as if he was about to blow a fuse.

'What the fuck are you lot doing in here?' he asked me. 'You're not from round these parts.'

'We don't want any mither,' I told the fella. 'We're just having a quiet drink. We're not here for all of that.'

Scotty didn't look too happy but, then again, there wasn't all that much he could do. There were eight of us and one of him and I was fucked if I was going to let him bully us out of the pub. We stayed exactly where we were until it was time for us to make our way to the ground.

After the match, we had a couple of beers and then we started strolling through the town to find another boozer. We managed to find a decent-enough spot to drink at and settled down there for a few more pints. I was in the toilets having a piss when the same irate-looking hooligan came striding through the door, running his mouth off at me.

'Whenever you're ready, dickhead,' he snarled.

'Eeyah mate, leave it out,' I said. 'We just want to drink our drinks and head off home in peace.'

'You're not getting out of here alive,' Scotty threatened. 'I don't give a fuck what you're here for.'

At this point, I was beginning to get a little bit worried. I knew that their firm would be out in force after the match and I didn't want a bunch of troublemaking wankers to ruin things for us. It was time for me to warn the rest of the Whites that we might get a twatting.

Scotty left the toilets, scowling and muttering to himself, and I finished off my piss and made my way back into the main room of the pub. We were going to have to come up with a plan of escape or we could end up getting leathered.

As soon as I arrived back at our table, the other Walkden Whites sensed that something was amiss.

'What's the matter?' one of my mates asked. 'You look a little bit worried.'

'It's that knobhead from the pub earlier,' I explained to him. 'He's just offered me out.'

'That doesn't sound too good,' my mate told me. 'There's a good twenty to thirty of them sat about outside. I'll tell you what we can do, though. There's another door over there and we can get the landlady to unlock it for us and sneak out round the side. That way, they'll be waiting around for us all night and we'll already have fucked off.'

He hadn't banked on the landlady being a complete and utter bitch. She refused to help us out and told us that we deserved as good as we got for going out drinking in Shrewsbury on a match day.

'You should have gone home earlier, you Bolton bastards,' she sneered. She was practically rubbing her hands together in anticipation of us getting battered.

'Right,' I said. 'There's only one thing for it. We're going to have to walk out through the middle of them. If we get away then we'll have done well for ourselves. Good luck everybody. Fingers crossed . . .'

Shrewsbury's mob were clearly going to hang about until we left the pub and we couldn't wait around forever. It was time for us to make our move, for better or for worse.

The minute we left the pub, Scotty and his boys were up off their seats, following us through the town. They walked right behind us for a good ten minutes and then they suddenly started giving chase. Everybody scattered and it was a game of cat and mouse until we got back to the station. Luckily, none of the group were particularly badly hurt. A couple of people got a slap and a kick here and there but we could have ended up a damn sight worse off. We had taken a major gamble by leaving the safety of the boozer to head off home and it had just about paid off.

We were relieved to have made it back to Bolton in one piece. We'd gone out expecting to have a couple of beers with a group of fellow Bolton supporters and we'd been kicked off on for no apparent reason. Shrewsbury's English Border Front were a load of fucking wankers. Dougie and the lads would never dream of laying into a group of shirt-wearing Shrewsbury fans so what gave them the right to start a fight with us? They are a bunch of bullying pricks and they tried their hardest to ruin our day out.

Shrewsbury's payback came a good five years later, in Sweden of all places. We had travelled over there to see the 1992 European Championships and stopped off for a drink in one of the local boozers. Me and a lad called Terry M were in the toilets having a slash when we noticed somebody putting up a sticker saying, 'Shrewsbury Town – English Border Front'. Now where had I seen this fella's ugly mug before? That's when it hit me. It was Scotty. Only this time round he didn't have his mates with him.

'Right, the minute everybody else has fucked off, shut that door and I'll say hello to our friend here,' Terry whispered over to me.

I nodded in agreement, fully aware of what he was about to do. Two minutes later, the leader of the so-called English Border Front was getting the beating of his life.

'Remember that,' yelled Terry, as he delivered one last punch to a confused and frightened-looking Scotty. 'This is from Bolton.'

It had been a fair few years since the original attack and Shrewsbury's firm were probably sitting around, scratching their heads and thinking, 'What did we do to piss the Bolton supporters off?' It just goes to show you that karma will always catch up with you, no matter how long it might take. It was a sweet revenge and I was glad that I was there to witness it. There is a major difference between somebody who fights with people who have travelled to a game for a scrap and somebody who is willing to kick off on a group of random fans.

Scotty and his crew overstepped the mark.

The Walkden Whites will always do their level best to avoid a confrontation, even when it looks as if there is no alternative. They could have had a row with Shrewsbury's mob but instead they tried to leave the pub without being drawn into a fight. They only resorted to violence after being attacked for no good reason.

The football-intelligence officers don't seem capable of making the distinction between the Bolton fans who are vocal in their support of their team, but yet 100 per cent peaceful, and hardcore hooligans like the Cuckoo Boys. Colin was arrested yet again in July 2010, after travelling up to Falkirk to watch a friendly. Central Scotland police accused him of breaking his banning order and locked him up for the night.

'Anyone who is subject of a banning order can expect to be dealt with robustly and that will ultimately mean spending the night or the weekend in police custody,' Deputy Area Commander Graham Taylor told the press.

The case against Colin was eventually dropped after it was deemed that his banning order only applied within England and Wales. That's what you get when you attempt to ban somebody from football for no reason. You end up wasting valuable police resources and you are made to look a fool in front of the entire country. Colin 1, Central Scotland police 0. Here's a tip: next time try going after somebody who is actually breaking the law.

10
FOREIGN SHORES

If you think that the Old Bill over here are bad then you want to see what they're like in some of the places on the Continent that we've been to. There are certain parts of the world where they like to crack skulls first and ask questions later. Human rights and civil liberties only really exist in the richer parts of Western Europe, as I'm sure that anybody who's ever travelled abroad to watch their team can attest to.

The Spanish coppers have been repeatedly criticised throughout the years for the heavy-handed way that they police football. In November 2004, the *Daily Telegraph* reported 'indiscriminate assaults on English fans by baton-wielding police' during a friendly in Madrid and, in April 2007, *The Independent* carried an article in which claims were made that the local coppers had assaulted a disabled Tottenham supporter during the UEFA Cup final. Whereas the majority of football fans would be put off travelling to a country with such a violent Old Bill, one of our members cites them as the reason that he enjoyed his trip so much. But then again, a run-in with the plod is very similar to a run-in with a rival set of hooligans.

Here's Phil to tell you why he prefers the Spanish approach to crowd control . . .

Phil

When I went over to Madrid in 2008 for a UEFA Cup tie with Atletico, I knew exactly what I was letting myself in for. The local coppers had smashed

United's fans to bits when they played at Barcelona in 1984 so I was expecting more of the same. Whenever English clubs play in Spain, the Old Bill knocks seven bells out of us. It comes with the territory; it is part and parcel of going over there.

There were a couple of minor scuffles before we even got inside the ground. The coppers were baton-charging all and sundry and there were dogs and horses running around all over the place. We had taken a load of lads across with us and we had some proper naughty boys on our side so we were fully equipped for whatever came our way.

The dibble were indiscriminately battering people, regardless of whether they were causing any trouble and some of them were even taking run-ups to baton us. I got baton-charged all the way into the ground, which was a bit annoying because I had paid €34 for a ticket and ended up getting in for free.

Inside the stadium, the coppers carried on brutalising anybody who got in their way. Even the stewards have got truncheons over there and they were joining forces with the plod to do us in. They had these weird-looking beige uniforms on and they were whacking anybody and everybody.

As soon as the match had kicked off, people started throwing coins around, which spurred on the Old Bill to hit us even harder. They were lashing out for fun and you could tell that they were enjoying themselves. We were fighting back as best we could but there is nothing worse than scrabbling about between the seats to get at someone and it was difficult to stay on our feet.

We had it with the coppers all the way through the game. I wasn't paying attention to what was happening on the pitch, as the action in the seats was far too exciting. Missiles were flying around all over the place and people were hurling anything and everything at the heavy-handed Spanish dibble. Chairs were being uprooted right, left and centre and the stadium descended into complete chaos.

By the time the match had finished, we were a little bit tired of it all. We'd probably had at least two hours of it. It wasn't just the ninety minutes of play because we had a good half hour of fighting before we got inside the ground. Piles of battered bodies lay stacked on top of one another, with the coppers laying into whoever was on top. I put my hand up to protect my face and felt my thumb immediately dislocate as a heavy metal truncheon hammered down into it. My entire thumb was now inverted. The way it was pointing was the opposite of what nature intended.

Yours truly on the legendary Manny Road.
It was our favourite place to attack opposition mobs.

Bolton violence didn't start with the era of the casuals.
We have been at it for decades . . . and always hounded by the Old Bill,
as this photo from the early Seventies shows.

Hull was always a moody place to go and when we went there on FA Cup business in 1984 it kicked off big time.

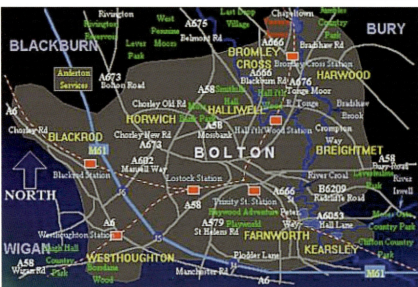

Top: This photograph of Burnden Park will bring back happy memories for so many of a Bolton persuasion.

Middle: The map shows the different areas of the town, and nearly every one of them has its own firm. Come match day, however, we fought under the Cuckoo Boys banner, for the whole of Bolton.

Right: Our calling card, which some of our lads actually got nicked for carrying.

Typical scenes from Bolton town centre in the Eighties as the opposing firms weigh each other up.

Away to Blackpool in 1988. The death of a young Tangerines fan at a Blackpool–Bolton game in 1974 means that every subsequent fixture between the two sides is fraught with danger.

We turned out in numbers for the visit of Middlesbrough in the mid-1980s.

We played Burnley at home in the mid Eighties
and their mob plotted up in the Bradford Arms.
We duly attacked but they cowered under the tables
and refused to come out.

This photograph was taken especially for this book on the Manny Road in the summer of 2010. It sums up the pride that every Bolton lad has in his team and his country.

At Thirsk, on our way to Middlesbrough.

Having a few pints before an EDL march.

Into Europe

Above: Bolton's game with Lokomotiv Plovdiv in September 2005 was not only the club's first game in Europe but also one of the most violent encounters we have ever experienced off the pitch.

Below: Face in the crowd. Marseille away in the 2006 UEFA Cup was also a dangerous sortie. We didn't exactly get a warm welcome from the French.

Bolton Youth

Above: The young lads have built up a great reputation for themselves in the last few years. Here they are having infiltrated Blackburn's end.

Below: Their numbers are growing all the time, as this photo shows.

England

Most of us have gone with England at one time or another.
Above: At an England–Holland game we ended up fighting with Chelsea.
Below: In a pub in Lancaster, on our way to take on the Jocks at Hampden.

Wanderers count the cost of mindless damage

Bolton blast lout fans

By GORDON SHARROCK

BOLTON Wanderers are teaming up with police in a fresh bid to beat the Burnden Park yobs.

A new wave of hooliganism has hit the club, prompting a high-powered initiative by the authorities.

Wanderers are counting the cost in cash of "mindless damage" inside the ground and are worried that a rising tide of racial problems will seriously damage their image.

Bananas were thrown onto the pitch in racial taunts aimed at Blackpool players Tony Cunningham and Steve Morgan last Saturday when a section of Wanderers supporters damaged seats and broke down a door in the Burnden Stand.

Both the club and Police, who held an emergency meeting on Tuesday believe the tide of hooliganism has stemmed from the fact that they have driven a massive wedge between rival fans, wiping out trouble between rival supporters inside Burnden Park.

"The Blackpool supporters were as good as gold, they didn't cause us a bit of trouble," Wanderers secretary Des McBain said today.

"But our own idiots were crazy. They got into the Burnden stand from the terrace, climbing in and breaking a door, and damaged seats.

"They are wrecking the chances of the club progressing. The money we are having to spend because of them could have gone to Phil Neal to spend on his team."

Supt Brian Swayles, second in command of Bolton Police says extra officers will be drafted in to tackle the problem of keeping the fans in check.

The racial problem will be dealt with separately. Police have already started the process of identifying the culprits and prosecutions could follow.

"I was not at the Blackpool game but I am told one or two bananas were thrown," he explained.

"This is not funny - it is disgusting behaviour which brings shame on the Borough. We know it has happened at other grounds but it has never happened here before."

DES McBAIN – appalled at the louts actions

> Over the years the press have always taken a great interest in our exploits. No one told me about the hit on Cantona. If I had known I would have thrown in a few quid!

Eight Whites fans banned from matches

by Edward Chadwick

EIGHT Bolton Wanderers fans have been banned from football matches since the start of this season in a crackdown on soccer thugs.

The ban means they cannot attend any club or international games.

The government announced earlier this year that instead of being issued with cautions or fixed-penalty notices for crimes related to football disorder — such as breaking windows or using threatening behaviour — fans would be taken to court and given football banning orders.

The move is designed to stop trouble at next year's World Cup in Germany.

And police warned today that known offenders would be targeted.

have revealed that a record number of hooligans are now subject to banning orders — a total of 3,153.

More than 1,000 were issued last year and among those who were banned were 12 Bolton Wanderers fans.

Police chiefs in Bolton today vowed that anyone who caused trouble at football matches would face a ban.

"We will not tolerate anyone who wants to cause a nuisance either around the Reebok Stadium or when they follow Bolton around the country," said PC Adie Ollerton, Bolton football intelligence officer.

"We are working closely with other forces and divisions and use plain clothes spotters to root out World Cup and the authorities are keen to make sure that anyone who causes problems in this country is not allowed to travel abroad."

The national figures also showed arrests for football-related offences dipped 11 per cent to 3,628 in 2004/05.

The number of arrests at league matches were the lowest since records began.

A total of 27 Wanderers fans were arrested at home and away matches last season — a rise of two on the previous season.

Anyone served with a banning order under the Football Disorder Act, which can last for two to 10 years, faces prison if they enter any ground in England or Wales.

Banned supporters must surrender their passport

YOBS IN £10,000 CONTRACT TO 'GET' CANTONA

We've been told, say police

EXCLUSIVE BY ALAN NIXON

POLICE have been warned that Eric Cantona could be the target of a bizarre plot to beat him up.

They are investigating reports that thugs have had a whip-round and the £10,000 "pot" will go to the one who attacks the Frenchman.

The claim has surfaced in Bolton, where Manchester United play tomorrow.

Inspector Graham Robertson, one of the officers in charge of security at the match, confirmed last night: "We have heard there is a whip-round available for the man who attacks Cantona. Too many people know about these situations as the word is going to Japan. We've had a sick joke on it doesn't, but we are convinced that the sub-claims have not gone away."

Police were last night considering changing the route taken by United's coach.

Cantona, who faces a late fitness test on his damaged thigh, has behaved impeccably since returning to the side after his knee-jerk ban.

But he is still the target for abuse and United have taken massive security measures to keep fans away from him.

HOT TROUBLE

Wanderers face fine over fans' flares at cup match

by Edward Chadwick

TWO Bolton Wanderers fans who let off flares during the club's UEFA Cup clash in Bulgaria today face a ban from European...

TAKE IT BACK, LAWRO: Dougie Mitchell, pictured with tattooist Fred Ivill

I've got you under my skin

By Alison Barton
abarton@boltoneveningnews.co.uk

BOLTON Wanderers fan Dougie Mitchell has certainly let Mark Lawrenson get under his skin.

The TV football pundit said he would shave off his moustache if the Wanderers stayed in the Premier League.

Lawro's moment of truth came on Friday at a posh London salon, but in anticipation, local artist Kevin Collins designed a cartoon of a terrified Mark being shaved by Wanderers boss Sam Allardyce.

Dougie was so impressed, he vowed to add the design to his collection of tattoos to raise money for Bolton Hospice.

He said: "It all started as a joke in the pub. When I saw the cartoon on the back page of the Bolton Evening News I told my friends I had thought about having it reduced and done as a tattoo on my back.

"A friend said I should have it done full size and I thought 'Why not! I could do it for charity'."

Not one to back out of a challenge, Dougie, aged 41, was duly inked during a two and half hour sitting by tattoo artist Fred Ivill, at Albert Road Tattoo Studio, Farnworth.

Lorry driver Dougie, of Starling Road, Farnworth, said: "I have lost count of how many tattoos I've got, but it's worth having this one to raise money for a good cause.

"My friends and family think I'm potty but my wife, Diane, is used to it now."

Fred, who has been tattooing for 25 years, was only too pleased to copy Kevin's design for the tattoo, and offered his services for free to help Dougie raise money.

He has been a Wanderers fan since childhood, and once helped save the life of a man at a match as he choked on his false teeth.

His artistic charity drive can still be sponsored, and the person pledging the most money will win a signed Wanderers shirt. For more information contact Bolton Hospice on 01204 520040.

Violence at the Hibs match caught on CCTV

Investigators to look at footage in bid to catch ringleaders

by Paul Keaveny
Crime Reporter

POLICE are scouring CCTV footage to identify the yobs who sparked violent clashes at Bolton Wanderers' pre-season friendly against Hibernian.

Riot police were called in when football fans clashed at the Reebok Stadium on Saturday.

Mounted officers rode in to quell trouble as supporters caused havoc in Middlebrook Retail Park, while others fought in the street in Stoneclough Road near Kearsley Station.

Chief Superintendent George Fawcett, the match commander, said: "Football intelligence officers are reviewing CCTV footage from both the stadium and from the evidence gathering teams who were at the scene.

"We will be working with our colleagues in Scotland to identify those responsible, seeking arrests or football banning orders where appropriate."

It is thought the disorder involved around 30 or 40 Bolton fans, many of whom were wearing England shirts.

As reported in The Bolton News yesterday, staff at

WORRYING SCENE: This picture of police separating fans leaving the Bolton v Hibernian match at the Reebok Stadium was taken by a fan caught up in the violence

Middlebrook said a mob of around 30 angry fans, understood to be Hibernian supporters, attacked shoppers and smashed windows.

Meanwhile, outside Kearsley train station, a group of about 40 Hibernian fans were returning to their minibus when fighting broke out. Lee Charlton, landlord of the Hare and Hounds, said about 100 people arrived in black taxis to attack the Scottish fans and vandalised their minibus.

It is thought that some of the fighting was pre-arranged and involved organised "firms" from Oldham, Bolton and Manchester. Two people were arrested at the scene. No-one was seriously injured.

Police had been tipped off that trouble was planned, and undercover spotters were employed to look out for early warning signs.

Trouble started during the second half of Jussi Jaaskelainen's testimonial game, when the atmosphere turned sour as fans' taunts turned into sectarian chanting, and rowdy supporters were escorted from the ground by police.

pkeaveny@theboltonnews.co.uk

With my son, Dean, outside Burnden Park.
This was after Bolton had played its final fixture there
but we will always have great memories of the old ground.

I am a plasterer by trade and my hands are essential for me to earn a living so I knew that if I didn't get myself sorted, I'd be fucked. The harder I struggled to disentangle myself from the heaving mass of bodies, the more my thumb began to hurt. It was fucking agony and, by this stage, I was panicking. I was in a massive amount of pain, I could hardly breathe and I was stuck.

Once I finally managed to extract myself from the heap, my first priority was to get out of the ground. I grabbed the nearest Old Bill and held my thumb up for him to see, as if to say, 'I've had enough, you can stop batoning me now.' The copper looked bemused.

'Hospital,' he told me. 'You need to go to hospital.'

It was quarter past eleven at night, I had no idea where the hospital was and I could hardly speak a word of Spanish. Some help he was.

I ended up going back to the hotel to try and pop my thumb back in myself. I filled the bath with warm water and I held it underneath the surface while I was doing it, under the logic that it wouldn't hurt as much if I kept it warm. After several failed attempts to fix myself, I eventually gave in. I was going to have to ride it out until we arrived back home in Bolton. I was in a horrendous amount of pain but there was nothing I could do about it. It was just a case of patiently holding on until I could get it seen to.

The following morning, I got up nice and early and headed off to the airport, where we were due to catch a flight to Barcelona. We had four hours to spare before our departure time so we decided to have our breakfast in a nearby McDonald's. That turned out to be a big mistake, because we somehow managed to stay there past the time that our plane was due to leave and had to catch a train instead.

Barcelona is a good five hundred miles from Madrid and I was in excruciating pain the whole way there. Everybody else was getting wrecked and drinking away, which made me feel even worse. I felt like a right killjoy but my thumb was fucking killing me and I really didn't want to be there.

By the time I finally arrived back in Bolton, I was fucking knackered. I'd had to endure a night of attempting to pop my thumb back in, a train journey halfway across Spain and a two-hour flight from Barcelona. Going to the hospital could wait. It was time for me to get some sleep.

At seven o'clock the following morning, I went to accident and emergency and explained to the doctor what had happened.

'You'd never have been able to click it back into place yourself,' he told me. 'You'd have been probing and probing but you need a trained professional to fix a dislocated thumb. Now sit back and relax, I'm going to give you some laughing gas to take away the pain.'

Fuck me, that laughing gas is powerful stuff. In the space of thirty seconds, I went from being in severe discomfort to giggling away to myself and feeling high as a kite.

'Have you started yet?' I asked the doctor.

'It's all done and dusted,' he told me.

I couldn't believe it. I hadn't felt a thing. I don't know why women are always going on about how painful giving birth is when they are pumped full of gas. I was away with the fucking fairies.

I wasn't the only person that ended up getting injured in Madrid. There were people with staples in their heads, stitches all over their bodies, the lot. At the end of the day though, nine out of ten lads would take a good hiding over a charge sheet any day of the week. You can criticise the Spanish coppers all you want but I was misbehaving and I deserved to get a beating. Fair enough they were heavy-handed but being smashed about the place with a truncheon beats ending up in a Spanish jail whichever way you look at it. If only the English coppers would follow their example.

He's right in a way. I preferred it in the days when the coppers would be content with giving you a clip around the earhole and sending you on your way. The foreign Old Bill might be a little on the thuggish side but, then again, you've got to look at the type of people they're dealing with.

When you're in another country, hooliganism takes on another dimension and, in certain places, the coppers are the main threat, whereas in others, they are the least of your worries. At some international games, we've had to venture into the moodiest terrain imaginable and have been relieved to come out of the other side in one piece. Fair enough you don't want to get locked up in a foreign nick but, at the same time, there are far scarier people than the plod out there.

One of the most dangerous places that I've ever followed Bolton to is a large, deprived city in the south-east of Bulgaria called Burgas.

It suffers from a range of social problems, including prostitution, organized crime, unemployment and drug abuse. It is basically the Liverpool of Eastern Europe.

'Although the town sits on the Black Sea coast, which is becoming increasingly popular with British tourists, Burgas still bears the scars of communism, with crumbling tower blocks dominating the skyline and much of the town run by the mafia,' wrote the *Bolton Evening News* in the run up to the game. 'The Foreign and Commonwealth Office (FCO) warns all travellers that low-level crimes, including pick-pocketing and carjacking, are rife, with foreign tourists often the targets.'

It is also where I got to know Graham, one of Bolton's top youth lads. He has agreed to have his account of the game included on the condition that I leave it exactly as he wrote it . . .

Graham

Our game against Plovdiv Lokomotiv in September 2005 was a trip I will remember for a long time, not only for the eventful things that happened and the fact that it was the first European game in Bolton's history but also because it was the game where I got friendly with some of the older Bolton lads for the first time. Until that point, I had been trying to get into the scene but I had not yet met the right people. Dougie Mitchell was one of the people I met and our friendship was built upon that game.

We decided to book a week in Bulgaria because it worked out cheaper than going for three days, what with the airlines and travel agents trying to rip every cunt off just because they knew that everyone was going over for the match. We stayed in a resort called Sunny Beach at a five-star hotel. The hotel was nice but outside was an absolute shithole. There were four- and five-star hotels all over the place, surrounded by utter poverty. The first thing that crossed my mind was that we were going to get robbed to fuck out there. It was the equivalent of someone in England trying to make Moss Side a tourist destination and putting hotels and tourists with loads of cash there. End result: some fucker's gonna get deprived of his wallet. The place was full of gypsies and rogue taxi drivers, who we had been warned not to trust because a lot of people had got into their cabs and been driven onto the hills, robbed at gunpoint and left there. This was advice from the receptionist at our hotel, who also told us, 'Whatever you do, don't walk home at night.' Well how the fuck are you supposed to get back if you can't walk or get a taxi? Fucking fly?

We experienced just how callous and impoverished these people were when, the night before the game, a group of gypsies shouted towards a group of eight of us, asking if we wanted any prossies. Dougie replied that he was gay to get them off our backs – but what happened next will live with me forever. The gypsy turned, went round the corner, came back with a small boy and shouted, 'Hey gay man! Gay man, for you.' Shocking. The one good thing about the place was that it was cheap as fuck. 38p for a pint of lager. Can't argue with that.

The day of the game came and all the Bolton fans in Sunny Beach met at a pub called the Happy Duck and occupied a number of other pubs on the beachfront. My friend and I had no idea how we were getting to the game, and we didn't even have tickets at that point, but luckily the word soon got round that one of the Bolton lads had hired a coach. We were asked if we wanted seats, as there were still some left. We jumped at the chance to get on board, although it ultimately resulted in us missing all the fun and games in Burgas, the town where the match was being played.

The game had been switched to a neutral stadium due to the fact that CSKA Sofia were also at home that night in the UEFA Cup. There would have been four thousand Bolton fans staying in Sofia if the game had been in Plovdiv, as the two cities are relatively near to one another. There would have no doubt been bedlam if this had happened.

Rumour has it that some of the Bolton lads had arranged to meet up with the local Burgas hooligans and join forces to attack Plovdiv, who were coming in by train. In fact two Bulgarians were seen talking and exchanging numbers the night before the game with the Bolton lads in the Happy Duck. Unfortunately, as is usually the case with Bolton, we couldn't organise a piss up in a brewery and fifty or so lads ended up in Burgas to take on a massive mob while the rest of us got on the coaches, which went straight to the ground. It was a joke. The lads on the coaches knew the plan but for whatever reason chose not to go.

From what I heard, Plovdiv had a fair mob in Burgas and it was a bit dodgy to say the least. Part of me was relieved to be safe and in the ground but part of me was pissed off at missing it. Like any foreign mob, they didn't have the class that English mobs have. We were told that they slapped a Bolton fan (who was with his son and wearing a Bolton top) after he offered them a handshake. When we returned home, photos of this assault on a harmless man with his son were posted on the internet, showing boots flying in and the victim on the ground. Like I say; no class.

The match was superb. We won 2–1 and nothing can describe the feeling after we scored the winning goal. We were sat twenty rows from the front but after the goal celebrations died down, we were right up against the fence at the front. It was mental. It was also nice to taunt their fans, who were ballooning all game and fighting among themselves at one point.

We returned to Sunny Beach after the game and began drinking in the Happy Duck. It started to quieten down after a while, as a lot of people had early flights in the morning, but we stayed out, as we were there for a few more days. We bumped into some lads from Breightmet and Little Lever, where I went to school, and they were heading over to a club on the strip along from the Happy Duck so we decided to join them.

About ten to fifteen of us went into a place called XL Disco. Within thirty seconds of us being in there, two of the lads who are well renowned for it dropped their trousers and started waving their dicks about. The locals weren't best pleased and we were ushered out. As we were leaving, one of the bouncers pulled something out of his pocket and we heard one of the lads scream and drop to the floor. I noticed that the bouncer had a stun gun in his hand and remember thinking, 'Fucking hell, they don't use them in Ikon[5].' The bouncer started advancing towards us with the gun but, unbeknown to him, one of the willy wavers snuck up behind him and gave him a crack to the side of the face. Two more bouncers arrived, making three in total. We immediately set about them before any more stun guns could be produced and backed them off into the doorway of the club, which had a huge glass front. We then got tables, chairs and glasses from the nearby restaurants, which were closed for the night but had left their furniture out. We bombarded the club, smashing the two big glass doors.

After running out of missiles, we started kicking and smashing a small concrete wall that lined one of the fountains on the strip. We removed blocks of

---

[5] A large nightclub in Bolton town centre.

paving from the top and smashed them up into smaller pieces on the ground. We then pelted the entire club front and struck a few bouncers in the process.

After a short while, the bouncers from the other clubs got wind of what was going on and piled down, getting us on our toes. We went to a nearby bar where a lot of Bolton lads were drinking and told them what had happened. We looked all set for a royal rumble of an off because these bouncers were well pissed off and we were fuelled by an all-day drinking session and the events earlier in the day in Burgas. However, by the time we got everyone back out onto the strip, the police were running round cracking people and some very pissed-off bouncers and locals were roaming round with machetes, coshes and bats. They started chasing us and everybody scattered.

Me, my mate, one of the willy wavers and one of Bolton's prominent black lads were chased by a mob of cosh-wielding policemen and machete-wielding bouncers. Not a good combination! We just about managed to lose them and get away, although the black lad was very nearly tripped by one of the coppers. That's how close it was.

We stopped at the end of the strip near the beach for a breather and the four of us agreed to split up and fuck off in different directions to avoid being hunted down by the mob. At this point, my mate turned to me and said, 'Fucking hell, I didn't know you could run that fast.' This was after I'd outrun him on the strip, him being a ten stone, fit-as-a-fiddle whippet and me being a fifteen-stone fat cunt with chronic asthma.

'I'd win Olympic gold if they put those cunts behind me at the start,' I said.

Upon returning to our hotel, we had a chance to reflect on what had gone on that night and realised the possible implications of our actions. About two months beforehand, a young Liverpool fan was sentenced to fifteen years in a Bulgarian jail for an alleged attack on a waiter after watching the Champions League final in a bar in Bulgaria. He was accused of leaving the barman with a fractured skull. It dawned on me that during our drunken rampage on the strip, one of the bouncers could easily have fallen victim to the same sort of injury as the barman, resulting in us looking at fifteen years apiece in a foreign hellhole. It was a sobering thought.

And if Graham's story doesn't prove to you what a bunch of fucking nutters our younger lot are then I really don't know what would. The Bulgarians probably didn't know what hit them. It takes a lot of guts to go over to an impoverished country like that and kick off with the local bouncers and I've got to give him credit for that.

Whereas the bouncers at the Bulgarian nightclubs would only get aggressive with people that were getting up to mischief, Lokomotiv Plovdiv's 'Lauta Hools' firm were a bunch of fucking bullies and had a reputation for going after regular, shirt-wearing fans. What they did to the father and his son outside the ground was unforgivable.

We were warned about Lokomotiv's mob by a group of hooligans affiliated with their rival team, Botev Plovdiv. We'd arranged to meet up with the Botev lads over the net and they seemed to have a very low opinion of the Lauta Hools.

'We call them gypsies because they are scruffy,' they told us. 'You have big firm. I think only Levski Sofia Hools would be big enough to take you on.'

Sofia is the largest city in Bulgaria so I took that as a compliment.

Botev's lads were proper sound and even taught us how to insult our rivals using the local lingo. By the time we'd finished drinking with them, I knew how to say 'gypsies' and 'cock-sucking motherfuckers' in Bulgarian.

It was little wonder that the other mobs all referred to Lokomotiv as gypsies, as they were a right scruffy bunch. I remember when we first caught sight of them outside the train station in Burgas city centre. It was the day of the match and seventy of their lads were getting off the train, dressed in their team colours and looking as if they hadn't had a bath for a good couple of years. There were only seven of us there and they could have easily battered us but for reasons best known to themselves they chose to do fuck all.

'Fuck this,' I told the rest of our lads. 'Let's go up the road towards the pub.'

We had expected there to be a couple more of our boys drinking in the boozer but there were only locals and shirters in there and I was beginning to think that we'd dropped a bollock by stopping off in the centre rather than getting a taxi directly to the ground. We were on our own in a hostile environment and I was feeling decidedly uneasy.

We carried on further up the street in the hope of finding the rest of our firm and we eventually bumped into a table full of lads from

West Houghton outside one of the pubs. I figured that we would be better off with a couple of extra faces with us so we joined up with them and headed off to the ground.

'You!' one of the Bulgarian Old Bill addressed us, as we walked past a group of the local coppers.

'You need to cross over the road when you get near main entrance of park.' We thanked him for his advice and continued on our way. Unbeknown to us, the copper had deliberately sent us off in the direction of Plovdiv's mob. There must have been a good two hundred and fifty of the fuckers and some of them were right big bastards. They were stood behind the railings at the side of the road, signalling that they were going to cut our throats and shouting, 'Die Bolton, die,' and 'Die English scum.'

'Stick together and stand your ground,' I told the rest of the firm. 'They won't all come.'

Only about thirty or forty of the Lauta lot looked like they were up for it.

'Not all of them are going to come,' I repeated. 'Stand!'

Two seconds later, the entire mob of Plovdiv were jumping over the railings to get at us and I was beginning to wish I'd kept my mouth shut. They pelted us with bricks and bottles and we backed off into the park, overwhelmed by their superior numbers.

For some reason, the Lautas Hools didn't follow us into the park. Maybe it was because they were a hundred-odd miles away from their patch and Burgas was just as alien to them as it was to us. Whatever the reason for their decision to hang back, they left us panicking in case they were suddenly going to change their minds and tear off after us.

We eventually came to a set of old railway tracks, which led us to a tennis court directly opposite to the stadium. There was another big mob of Plovdiv milling about outside but luckily for us there were a lot of our shirters around as well, which seemed to deter them. Once we were safely inside the ground, we were able to hook up with the rest of our firm and find out how they had fared against Plovdiv.

'We saw them on the way to the match and they were straight on their toes,' one of the lads filled me in. 'Some of them got legged into a block of flats and none of them stood. The fucking lot of them bottled it.'

It seemed as if the stories about the so-called Lautas Hools were true. They were only brave when they were picking off small groups of stragglers. When they were faced with a similar-sized mob to theirs, they had immediately buckled under the pressure and made a run for it.

The game itself was fairly uneventful. A small mob of Botev managed to get into the Lokomotiv end and we tried to get across to join them but the Old Bill all have guns over there so it wasn't happening. We beat the bastards 2–1 and the coppers locked us in the ground for an extra half an hour after the match had finished in the hope that it would prevent another disturbance.

Once we had finally been let out, we were held behind the gates at the main road leading back to town for another quarter of an hour. The Lautas Hools were nowhere to be seen. Botev had been spot on about them. They were a load of cowardly, scruffy wankers and they were only willing to fight when the odds were stacked firmly in their favour.

A couple of days later, Plovdiv's lads were posting bullshit about us on the internet, claiming they had done us. Two hundred and fifty of them had chased a handful of us off into a park but that was hardly something for them to be proud of. They're game as fuck when it comes to beating up shirters and picking on smaller groups of lads but when they're faced with an equal number of rival hooligans, they're a load of fucking fannies.

Our European games have been some of our most exciting as a mob, despite Plovdiv going on like a bunch of lying cunts the minute the match had finished. It is always a proper buzz to know that you've gone to somebody else's country and taken them on in their own backyard and to all of the people who say that hooligans aren't real football fans, how many of you would have risked getting your arses beaten by a mob of angry Eastern Europeans for the sake of upholding the pride of your team? Not very fucking many I'd say. We even managed to smuggle a flare into the ground to demonstrate our support.

The local papers had a fucking field day over the flare incident, running an article that showed a picture of five excited-looking figures, silhouetted against the bright red light.

'The club is set to be hit with a fine from the UEFA chiefs

following an investigation,' wrote Edward Chadwick in the *Bolton Evening News*. 'Police in Bolton confirmed that they have identified two men from the video footage thought to be responsible for the incident. And they urged all Wanderers supporters to observe a ban on terrace fireworks and flares.'

Phil was one of those two men. Here's what he's got to say for himself about his antics in Bulgaria that day . . .

Phil

Plovdiv was my first European trip and I wanted something to mark the occasion. As far as I'm concerned, flares are the ultimate means of registering your support for your team and there is no better way of making your presence known than to light one during the match. As Dougie and Graham have already noted, Burgas was a proper dodgy place. The entire beachfront was full of stalls selling snide goods, pirate DVDs and dangerous-looking knives, which left no doubt in my mind that I'd be able to get my hands on some contraband pyrotechnics.

'I want some fireworks,' I told the owner of one of the beachside weapon shops. His store was filled to the brim with all manner of different knives and machetes and he definitely seemed like the type of person who could sort me out. He had big blades, small blades, straight blades, curved blades, CS gas, swords, you name it. If anybody could provide me with a flare it was going to be him.

'I no sell them,' the shopkeeper told me. 'Anything else you want?'

That was strange. He seemed to sell just about everything else.

'Okay I'll have some pepper spray, a retractable cosh and a couple of boxes of bangers,' I told him.

The entire lot came to the equivalent of £8, which cheered me up a little bit. I was gathering up my purchases ready to leave the shop when the fella started beckoning me closer to him, as if he wanted to tell me something before I went. Maybe he'd got some fireworks in after all.

'How many flares you want?' the geezer whispered.

'Do us ten,' I told him, brimming with excitement now that I was finally getting somewhere.

'Okay,' he said, 'but I can't sell now. Come back tomorrow and I have them here.'

I thanked the shopkeeper for his help and hurried off back to my hotel room, eager to check out my purchases. I needed all of the weapons that I'd got off him just to be able to walk around the city without the fear of getting robbed. It was a rough old place and there were menacing-looking gypsies mugging people all over the resort.

The CS gas and the cosh were proper handy but I still couldn't wait to get my hands on the flares and so, the following morning, I lit up a nice big spliff and headed off back to the weapon shop to see if the owner had got my order in.

'No, no, no!' he shouted at me, the minute I walked in through the door. 'Police see you, you go jail.'

Eh? Was he really trying to tell me that you could buy batons and machetes from your average run-of-the-mill shop but yet the coppers would haul you down to the station for smoking a little bit of weed?

'You fucking what?' I asked him, finding it difficult to believe what I was hearing.

'Jail,' he repeated. 'Police see you smoke, you go jail.'

I decided to take the fella's word for it and immediately stubbed out my spliff. After all, I didn't want to do anything that was likely to jeopardise my chances of getting the flares.

'Have you got them then?' I asked him, feeling as if I was a kid in a candy shop.

'Yes,' he told me, 'Here you go.'

Fucking get in! Now all that was left to do was for me to smuggle one of them into the stadium without the local Old Bill getting onto me.

I stashed a flare in one of my pockets, put a handful of bangers in the other and headed off to the match with the rest of our lads. We had a mission and a half on our hands to get to the ground. It was in the middle of the slums and we had to make our way past an eerie-looking abandoned hospital on our way there. It was covered in used bandages and looked like something out of a horror film.

As we approached the stadium, we saw five hundred big, meaty-looking, football lads getting off the train at the station. They were Plovdiv. We only had thirty-odd lads with us and to say that we were a little bit unnerved would have been the understatement of the century.

'Fucking hell, where's the dibble?' I asked one of my mates. 'Look how many of them there are.'

If that many hooligans had got off the train in Bolton, the Old Bill would have been there in a matter of seconds but, then again, we were in the middle of an Eastern European ghetto and the only law that mattered was the law of the person with the most men on their side.

We managed to get to the ground without Plovdiv's mob getting onto us but, to my dismay, a bunch of big, burly stewards were searching our fans on their way into our end. One of our lads got the contents of his pockets confiscated at the entrance and turned around to me to warn me that I wasn't going to make it in. 'Phil,' he said, 'You've got no chance, mate.'

I was crestfallen but I wasn't giving up that easily. I was going to get that flare into the stadium if it was the last thing I did.

'Right I'm not going to be able to get the flare and the bangers into the ground,' I whispered to one of my mates, ushering him on ahead of me as I spoke. 'You go in without me and I'll go round to the railings at the back of our end and pass them through to you. It's my only hope of getting them past the stewards.'

There was a set of steps leading up a grass embankment at the back of the ground and my intention was to go up, poke the contraband items through the fence and then go straight back down again. However, to my surprise, there were no Old Bill about at the top and there was an unlocked door leading into the stands. Why anybody bothered going in the front way was beyond me. I casually strolled in and positioned myself alongside the rest of our firm, taken aback at how easy it would have been to get in without a ticket if I hadn't already bought one prior to leaving England.

The match was being broadcast live on telly and we were all proper excited about it. The atmosphere was electric and now that I'd managed to get inside without having anything taken off me, the only thing that was needed to cap it off was for me to light my flare. But when should I spark it up? What was the best time to get it out? I didn't want to ruin my big moment after all the effort I had put in.

The minute it got to halftime, a set of flares went up all the way from one side of Plovdiv's stand to the other.

'Fucking hell,' I thought. 'You rum bastards.'

There were thick clouds of smoke billowing around the stadium and I couldn't have hoped for a better sign that the time was right for me to start my own personal light display.

Not wanting to be outdone by the locals, I whipped the flare out of my trouser pocket, lit the end and held it high above my head, spewing pieces of burning shit out onto the supporters who were nearby.

'Fucking hell, what are you doing there?' complained a pissed off Bolton fan.

Talk about ungrateful! A couple of hot rocks burning a hole in his shirt was a small price to pay for such a magnificent spectacle.

If I had lit up a pyrotechnic device in Bolton, I would have been shitting myself in case the coppers got onto me but the plus side of being in such a dodgy, corrupt country was that I knew full well the local Old Bill wouldn't bother to arrest me. They would just leather me! As I've said before, I'd take a beating over a nicking any day of the week and so there was nothing for me to worry about. I was free to bask in the glory of the bright red light that my contraband firework had produced to my heart's content.

The flare eventually burnt down to a stump and one of the lads held it between his fingers, pretending it was a cigarette. Now it was time for me to open up the bangers. I wouldn't say that they made a loud noise but they made just enough of a bang to make you jump and we took great delight in chucking them at the coppers. I ended up giving some to a lad called Jimbo and he pelted our fans with them. I guess that's what happens when these things get into the wrong hands!

Going to Bulgaria ranked alongside our Spanish adventure in terms of the amount of excitement that we experienced and the flares were the icing on the cake. The papers tried to pass our antics off as deliberate acts of defiance but, in reality, they demonstrated the extreme lengths that we were willing to go to in order to express support for our team.

We flew back home on the Friday and my memories of the flare weren't the only souvenirs that I had to remind me of my time in Burgas, as I managed to smuggle a cosh into England. It is relatively easy to bring a weapon with you on the plane. All you have to do is shove it in the middle of your luggage and nine times out of ten they won't pull you for it when it goes through the X-ray. It would've been a shame to leave all my purchases from the weapon shop in Bulgaria and it was something to remember my first European journey by.

The cosh was a very apt souvenir to bring back, as it was representative of the type of place that we stayed in. Mind you, the fact that Burgas was such a dodgy city was what had made our trip there so exciting. It was a journey into the unknown and each of our lads had their own personal adventure, whether it was legging it through a park with a couple of hundred rival hooligans in hot pursuit or sneaking pyrotechnics into the stadium. Bulgaria was one of many unforgettable times that we've spent together and it will go down in the annals of Cuckoo Boys history as another place we've left our mark on.

As well as following our beloved Bolton Wanderers to foreign shores, a couple of our lads have been involved in the England scene. Fighting abroad at an England match is a little different to fighting at a Bolton match, because it involves brawling away alongside members of rival English firms. It is a good way of making a name for yourself, as it can spread your reputation throughout the country and, of course, it's another excuse for travelling overseas with a big group of mates, which is always good in my book.

The action that we've been involved in at our games in European competition hasn't always involved rival hooligans. Sometimes we've ended up scrapping with the local nutters, as they've been the only ones that were up for it. That was the case when we played Olympique de Marseille in the 2006 UEFA Cup. I knew it would be hairy over there, having heard stories about North Africans giving English fans a hard time in the 1998 World Cup, when England played Tunisia in a group game. Still, lads from Farnworth, Walkden, Tonge Moor, Great Lever and Halliwell were all heading over for the game and I didn't want to miss out on the trip.

Marseille has had a large immigrant community ever since hordes of Italians and Greeks flocked to the city at the end of the nineteenth century. Although the majority of the ethnic population coexists fairly peacefully with the natives, there have been several high-profile race riots in recent years. It is a place that is often associated with crime, unemployment and social unrest and I was very apprehensive about travelling over there.

When we arrived on French soil, our hotel was a good twenty minutes walk from the centre so we dropped our belongings off and headed off to meet the rest of our fans at one of the local bars. There wasn't much to see or do so we figured that we'd get a couple of beers in with the boys to pass the time.

After having a bit of a natter and downing a few pints, we ventured out of the boozer and into this big concrete square with a fountain in the middle. Some of the lads started messing about in the water and clambering up onto the nearby statues, which seemed to shock the passers-by. We were always larking about with the fountains in Bolton town centre but the locals here didn't seem best pleased about it. They were looking at us as if we were a group of fucking mad men.

Our daft antics drew large crowds of Frenchmen to the square and gained a lot of unwanted attention so we decided to head off to the bars at the front of the marina to get a few more pints in. By this stage, we were all pissed up and a couple of the firm started lobbing chairs and bottles around the place. Before I knew it, the French Old Bill were on the scene and we were forced to retire to our hotel.

We were part way through the journey back to our digs when one of our younger lot came running round the corner to tell us that a group of older locals had been giving him shit.

'Right show me where they are,' I told him. This was the moment we had been waiting for. It was about to go off.

We followed the youngster back along the street and sure enough, a bunch of cocky-looking Frogs of North African descent were mooching about outside a seedy bar. As soon as they saw us coming, they got their mates out of the boozer and started advancing along the road towards us, signalling that they wanted to call it on. By this stage, we were pissed as fuck and a fair few of us were on the ching as well, which made us even more up for it. It was time for us to teach the cunts a lesson.

After the first couple of punches, the Frogs were on the back foot so we pelted them with the chairs from outside the nearby pubs as they retreated back inside the bar. We tried to follow them in but the doorman was built like a brick shithouse and he wasn't budging. A couple of projectiles were thrown in his direction but he stood his ground and refused to let us past.

Realising that the fella wasn't going to move, we decided to call it a day and set off back along the street towards our hotel. Part way through our journey a group of younger North Africans emerged from one of the side streets and started shouting abuse at us. We set off after them but they were straight on their toes and we decided not to follow them in case they were leading us into a trap. They could have been luring us into the area they lived in and I didn't want to end up in the middle of some hellish French ghetto, surrounded by knife-wielding Algerians and Moroccans.

We could hear sirens in the distance so we decided to split up into two separate groups in order to avoid getting nicked. I chose to go along with the smaller faction, which turned out to be a good decision, as the other group got ordered onto their knees by the Old Bill and clubbed around the head with truncheons. It was a narrow escape and it saved me waking up with a headache the next morning.

The following day, we headed back to the marina to meet up with the rest of our firm. We stood around discussing the previous night's shenanigans then set off to the match. The lads that had missed out on the action were proper envious of our run-in with the Africans and we were itching to have another go at them.

The game against Marseille in the Stade Vélodrome was proper atmospheric. They had MCs stood on giant industrial speakers, leading their fans in their chants, which would never have happened in Bolton – the stewards would have wet their fucking pants! Unfortunately, we lost the game by two goals to one and, after drawing the first leg in Bolton, we were eliminated. We were hoping to have it out outside the stadium with the locals but only a handful were up for it and they were quickly smashed to pieces. A couple of Frogs got dragged out of their cars and battered and a few shop windows went through but, apart from that, nothing of interest went off. We set off back to the marina to see if anything was happening there.

The locals didn't seem to be up for a fight so we went into a moody-looking underground nightclub filled with weed-smoking French Rastas, just for something to do. It was proper random but they didn't give us any trouble so we didn't bother them. I was disappointed that we hadn't got to have another row after the match but, at the same time, I was made up that it had kicked off with the

Africans beforehand. There was no sign of any French hooligans the whole time I was there so it was a good thing that the Moroccans and the Algerians were up for a scrap. They had made it a day to remember and if they hadn't turned out for us it would have been completely trouble free, which would have made it a wasted journey.

Spain, Bulgaria and France are three of the many places the Bolton boys have left their mark on. They won't forget us in a hurry and no doubt the next generation will invade countless other countries in the years to come. Our international games were a real test of our mettle. It's one thing scrapping with the supporters of a team who play a couple of hours down the road but when you're in somebody else's country with no way of getting back, you need to have your wits about you. Whether we were fighting with fellow hooligans, Bulgarian bouncers or North African Frenchmen, our foreign adventures were always fraught with danger and I wouldn't have wanted them to be any other way. We had some proper exciting times and hopefully there will be more to follow further down the line.

11
BRISTOL CITY

Much as I loved our run-ins with the foreign teams, it was equally pleasurable to stamp our authority on one of the more notorious English firms. Whereas certain mobs had managed to forge a reputation for themselves, others were still in the process of cementing their status and, throughout the mid 1980s, Bristol City's City Service Firm were looking very promising indeed. They were holding their own against the likes of Millwall and Portsmouth, who were both top five firms at the time, and they were rapidly becoming known as a mob to watch out for.

Here is what one of our Great Lever lads has got to say about the CSF . . .

GLL

I was proper made up when I found out that we were going up against Bristol in the Freight Rover Trophy final in May 1986. I had heard about their battles with some of the teams down south and I knew they would be worthy opponents. We were playing them at Wembley and decided to remain completely trouble free until we were in London, as we didn't want the Old Bill to get onto us before we arrived.

Leaving nothing to chance everything was planned out well in advance of the game. Some of the Tonge Moor lads had bought a load of train tickets using stolen credit cards, which meant that we didn't have to worry about getting to the stadium. We had arranged to get the overnight train from Manchester Piccadilly, arriving in the capital at around 5.30 a.m. and giving us plenty of time before the game kicked off.

All was going well until a couple of the firm decided to kick off on a load of random black lads at Piccadilly Gardens bus station. I wasn't there to see it but one of our lot ended up getting slashed and had to go to hospital. Our main boys weren't best pleased and the other lads who had been involved in the confrontation got a right bollocking.

'Save it for Bristol,' they were told. 'Are you trying to fuck this up before we've even set off? It'll be a shit day for you if you bring it on top with the Old Bill and I get pulled because of you, you stupid cunts.'

Luckily, we were able to make it onto our train without anything else going off and before we knew it, we were well on our way to London. The journey down was just like any other trip to an away game. People were taking the piss out of one another, some of the firm were ballooning about how hard they were and others were reminiscing back to their previous battles with Bristol, all of which were well before my time.

We had seventy-odd lads with us and Bolton had managed to get itself together over the previous year, culminating in all the component firms coming together as one. Our numbers usually ranged from twenty-five to two hundred-plus and the Tonge Moor Stanley Boys were easily the worst of the lot. They would go steaming into anybody who stood in their way and a lot of them tended to go to the games armed with knives and hammers, making them a valuable asset to our mob.

Our train pulled into Euston station directly on schedule and we set off to Borough Market on the tube. The boozers there all opened early to cater for the market workers and we figured that we might as well start the day off how we intended to continue. The landlord did a double take when seventy of us walked into his pub at six o'clock in the morning, ready to order lager after lager. Once we'd got the beers in and had a bit of time to settle down, the whiz came out. One of our main boys had a plentiful supply and we were necking it like it was going out of fashion.

By the time it got to nine o'clock, we were all pretty wired. We headed off to Trafalgar Square, where we met up with another thirty-five of our lads, who had come down on one of the later trains. We now had at least a hundred boys with us and it was time to cause some mischief.

Our initial plan to stay out of trouble was easier said than done. One of our lads robbed a load of beer from a shop and handed it out to everybody else and a lad called Brownie went around in a toy policeman's helmet, pretending to arrest the tourists. He was funny as fuck and we were all in stitches.

As the day went on, the main lads started getting serious, calming everybody down and making sure that everything was in place. We were originally planning on getting off the tube a station early and walking up to Piccadilly Circus but part way through our journey, there was a sudden yell of, 'They're here,' closely followed by 'There's fucking loads of them.' The next thing we knew, Bristol's notorious City Service Firm were storming along the street towards us.

'Wait until they're on top of us,' one of the senior figures in the firm instructed us.

There were at least a hundred and fifty of them and they looked to be a handy set of lads. I grabbed the metal insert out of a bin and carried it behind my back, attempting to conceal it so that I could launch it at them the minute they came within range.

Within a split second, the streets had descended into all-out warfare. Skirmishes flared up all across the road and the traffic came to a complete standstill. After a good five minutes of fighting, both mobs started backing away but as soon as we had regained our composure, we were straight back into them, laying into anybody who got in our way. I ended up getting a crack from the side and falling down onto my arse. By the time I was back up on my feet again, my attacker had managed to lose himself in the middle of their mob and I was sadly unable to return the favour.

We got at least ten minutes of rowing in before the coppers turned up in numbers, at which point we were forced to call it quits. The priority at this stage was for us to get away as quickly as we possibly could to avoid the Old Bill getting a grip of us. There would be time for a second round later in the day.

We arrived at Wembley at half-past one and by that stage, our mob had grown significantly. Lads had met up with us at various locations across the city and we had a fearsome set of boys at our disposal. We were running along the street, cheering our team coach as it arrived, when we spotted the City Service Firm walking towards us on the other side of the road. It had taken us a good couple of minutes to get onto them, as they were mixed in with the shirters, but as soon as we became aware of them, we were right in.

A horde of angry Bolton lads swarmed around the Bristol lot, mobbing them from the side as well as from the front and causing them to panic. This big fucker in a dark-coloured leather jacket was screaming for them to stand but only a handful of them paid him any mind. A good twenty CSF refused to be budged and we were left to fight their gamest set of lads.

The big fella was as hard as fucking nails. He refused to go down even when he had a full can of lager smashed into the side of his head. If their other lads had been as tough as he was they might have stood a chance, but, as it was, we ended up slapping them a good hundred metres up the road.

After a fair few minutes of going at it, the coppers eventually managed to get the situation under control and we made our way inside the stadium to watch the game. Some of our boys had missed out on the action so we filled them in on what had happened and they listened with envy in their eyes as we told them how the majority of Bristol's firm had run away. The battle wasn't over yet though; the post-match festivities were still to come.

Bolton won 3–0 but none of us stayed behind to watch the trophy being presented, as we were eager to find the Service Firm. We made our way over to their end and spotted them stood in front of the old twin towers at the top of Wembley Way. By this stage, we must have had at least two hundred lads with us. We had met up with the remainder of our firm during the match and we were like a proper fucking army. Bristol backed off. They didn't run; they just tentatively edged away. It was looking likely that we were going to win this round as well. We both had relatively equal numbers but we were far more up for it than they were and we soon got the upper hand.

The mounted police arrived on the scene fairly quickly and started twatting anybody that they could get their hands on. Two could play at that game. A mate of mine gave one of their horses a cracking right hook and it almost threw the rider off its back. We were fucking pissing ourselves. It was funny as fuck. The Old Bill eventually managed to box us off using horses, police bikes and vans and we were taken to a tube stop and left on the platform. Just as we were beginning to think that the action had finally come to an end, I heard one of our lads shouting a warning over that Bristol were there and saw a hefty mob of the fuckers coming down the stairs towards us.

'You cheeky cunts,' I thought to myself. 'We've just this minute done you.'

A couple of Bristol's frontline seemed up for it but the lads at the back of their mob couldn't see what was going on and didn't seem to be moving.

Luckily for them, a small group of coppers managed to get in front of them and escorted them back onto the upper level of the station. We half-heartedly pelted them with missiles as they went but we knew deep down there was no chance of having another battle with them.

Thinking that we'd seen the last of CSF, we got the train to Baker Street, where we needed to change to get to Euston. We were wandering around the station attempting to get our bearings when, lo and behold, Bristol's firm pulled in at a nearby platform. It was fucking unbelievable. We started hammering on the doors and windows of their carriage, desperately trying to get at them before their train started moving again. They were fucking shitting it.

Bristol's firm managed to hold the carriage doors shut just long enough for them to get away. We were deprived of the pleasure of battering them for a third consecutive time but we had already done them on numerous different occasions throughout the day so we were still proper made up. The CSF were a game set of lads so credit where it's due but they got a fucking hammering and we did ourselves proud.

There were a couple of rumours flying around during our trip home. Apparently, Millwall had been out in force and Bolton and Bristol had collectively turned them over, although I never saw any Bushwhackers about the place. The second rumour I heard was that some of Chelsea's firm were with us, which was a load of bollocks. We did have a slight connection to Chelsea during the 1980s, as one of our main lads knew a couple of their mob, but we certainly didn't take any of them with us to Bristol.

Rumours aside, it would be difficult for anybody to deny that we got a result that day. We ran the CSF lot ragged and proved that we were able to compete with the big boys. Bolton has never been one of the main firms, even in the Eighties when we were at our strongest, but we are definitely one of the best mobs in the north-west. The fact that we were able to come out on top against a set of lads that had been having it with the likes of the Millwall Bushwhackers and Portsmouth's 6.57 Crew speaks for itself. It was one of the best away games that I've ever been to and I was proper chuffed with the outcome.

It's little wonder there were stories going around speculating that we'd teamed up with Millwall. The Bushwhackers were one of the hardest firms going back then and Bristol must have thought that we were at a similar level to them. The CSF had held their own against Pompey and Millwall but it doesn't take a top five firm to turn somebody over, it takes a firm that are willing to stand their ground and Bolton were exactly that.

12
THE BAGGIES

The Midlands had some equally naughty mobs. The Baggies were notorious for their fearsome run-ins with Wolves and Villa and their Section 5 mob had been heralded as one of the best firms going. When P heard that we were going up against them in February 2003, he could hardly contain his excitement . . .

P

Fifty of our lads boarded the train to Wolverhampton with the intention of causing as much havoc as possible. We were planning on travelling to Wolves by rail and jumping in a taxi to Birmingham so that the Old Bill wouldn't get onto us, which meant that none of us were particularly keen on paying for a ticket. We'd be shelling out enough money as it was.

We managed to avoid the inspector for the first half of the journey but some of the younger lads were smoking weed in the toilets and he was alerted to their presence by the thick, black clouds of marijuana billowing out of the door. The driver wasn't best pleased with our behaviour and he stopped the train at some shitty little town in the middle of nowhere.

'Sling your hook or I'm calling the police,' he informed us.

Me and my mates stepped down onto the platform, thinking that the rest of our lads would follow, but the next thing we knew, the train had started up again. The remainder of the firm were sticking two fingers up at us out of the windows, clearly amused that we were getting left behind. We had to wait for the next train down to Birmingham. When we got to Brum the other Bolton lads were stood there waiting for us and they let out an almighty cheer. They seemed to think it was hilarious that we had been left behind and we got a fair bit of ribbing for it throughout the course of the day.

Now that we were reunited with the rest of our mob, it was time to get the beers in. We headed off to a nearby pub and made a beeline for the bar. Some of the staff looked a little bit on the poofy side so a few of our lads started wolf whistling and taking the mickey out of them, which caused one of them to call the pigs on us. It really wasn't our lucky day. The coppers turned up and started searching everybody, which was a cause for concern, as some of the lads had a bit of Charlie on them. A couple of us decided to make a run for it and we legged it through a nearby shopping centre with the plod in hot pursuit. We jumped into the back of a black cab and ordered the driver to take us straight to the Hawthorns, breathing a sigh of relief that the Old Bill hadn't caught up with us.

The taxi driver did as we commanded and we were soon safe inside the ground. The game itself was relatively uneventful. There was a good atmosphere but we drew 1–1 and nothing kicked off, which is always a bit of a disappointment. On our way out of the stadium, a couple of the West Brom lads were giving us a bit of shit through the big metal fence that separated our fans from theirs. We tried to reach through the railings to smack them but we ended up doing more damage to ourselves than we did to them.

After a couple of futile attempts to have it with the Baggies, we decided to call it a day and headed off to the Moat House hotel, where we had arranged to meet up with the rest of our mob. It was a fair walk from the ground and a couple of lads got separated from the main body of the group, which resulted in them getting picked off. This only added fuel to the fire and, by the time we got to the hotel, we couldn't wait to get into West Brom's firm.

We were sat around in the Moat House bar when a few of our younger members came running in, telling us that the Baggies had been giving them shit out the front. A couple of us ventured outside to have a look but by this stage it was dark and we couldn't see a fucking thing. We were just about to go back inside the pub when we heard a load of shouting coming from a small section of banking at the end of the car park, and, the next thing I knew, forty West Bromwich lads were charging towards us, wielding big fuck-off planks of wood.

The Section 5 lot were tooled up to fuck and managed to back us off into the doorway of the pub. Luckily, the rest of our firm had heard what was going on and they came running down the hallway to even up the odds. Now that we had a couple more lads at our disposal, we would show the Baggies a thing or two.

We flung open the door and it was our opponents' turn to back away. Then, as soon as they had regained their composure, they stormed across the car park towards us, flailing wildly with their planks of wood. One of their black lads twatted one of our lot round the head and blood started literally pissing out.

'Get the nigger,' shouted another of our lads, after seeing what had happened.

Our entire firm went crazy, launching themselves into the Baggies with all their might and causing them to drop their weapons and flee. We had a couple of black lads in our firm at the time and I can remember thinking that the choice of wording was a little bit over the top. Still, it did the trick. We were literally falling over one another to get at them and we took great delight in pelting them with bricks and bottles as they desperately struggled to get away.

The Old Bill turned up at the hotel shortly after our rivals had got off and demanded to know what had gone on. The lad that had been hit in the head with the plank of wood was bleeding quite profusely and it was blindingly obvious there had been a ruck.

'I've got no idea what happened,' I lied to the coppers.

The rest of the firm were just as uncooperative.

'Well seeing as you've all got temporary amnesia, we're going to have to escort you all back to the station,' one of the Old Bill told me.

It had been an action-packed day but it was finally time for it to come to an end. I was secretly hoping that our West Brom friends would try it on with us again on our way back but I think they must have had enough and called it a night by that stage because they were nowhere to be seen.

All in all, it was a proper good day out. We had got the better of the Section 5 mob even though they had been tooled up and are a game set of lads so it was no small feat. I would definitely rank them among the top Midlands firms. Getting a result against a mob like theirs made us feel proper chuffed with ourselves and helped to cement our reputation as a firm that couldn't be *intimidated. We had conquered an opponent in their own backyard in spite of the fact that they were all armed to the teeth and we had walked away with our heads held high.*

13
MIDDLESBROUGH

Middlesbrough is probably the roughest town we've been to. They don't fuck about in the North-East and their hooligans are no exception. Boro's infamous Frontline are one of the best mobs in the country, highly respected by everybody who has ever had a run-in with them. They're definitely a force to be reckoned with and many a team have come unstuck against them over the years, including Bolton in December 1978.

The game in question sticks in my mind because it was Boxing Day and we were all hung over from Christmas. I was feeling rough as fuck but after a quick hair of the dog and plenty of weed I felt shit hot again and couldn't wait to get to Boro. I was only seventeen at the time, and the youngest lad there, but I was just as up for it as the rest of our lads.

We had opted to travel to the match in a van and I was cramped up in the back with a load of cans and a spliff. It wasn't exactly roomy but I wasn't complaining. We had a pack of cards to entertain us and we were looking forward to getting stuck into the Boro lads once we had reached our destination.

We stopped off at a pub in Thirsk in North Yorkshire part way through our journey, which was a recipe for trouble, as one of us will usually end up kicking off with the locals wherever we end up. Sure enough, half an hour after we'd got there, one of our lot butted somebody in the face and it went off like fuck. This crazy Yorkshireman was twatting everybody about the place with a pool cue and it took about twelve pint pots to take him out of the picture.

After a brief scuffle, we ended up legging the locals out of the pub and chasing them across the square. A few of the drinkers came out of the nearby pubs to have a gander but they soon decided that they didn't want any and fucked off back to where they had come from. By this stage, we were beginning to worry that the Old Bill were going to turn up so we jumped back into our van and high-tailed it out of town, not wanting to end up getting nicked before we'd even got to Middlesbrough.

An hour and a bit later, we pulled up at the side of Ayresome Park and walked down to the ground, bristling with excitement at the thought of getting another row. There were a load of Frontline lads around but with coppers all over the place we had no chance of getting into them. Oh well, I thought to myself, we can always get at them after the game has finished.

Disappointed by the heavy police presence, we made our way into the ground and positioned ourselves in the left-hand corner, behind the goal. It ended up being a 1–1 draw, with Frankie Worthington scoring for us. Towards the end of the match, a message came over the tannoy, telling us that we were going to be escorted to our trains and coaches once the final whistle had blown.

'We're not going the same way as the escort,' one of our lads told a nearby copper, hoping that he'd leave us to our own devices. 'We came up here in a van and we're parked up at the side of the road, near the park.'

The Old Bill kept us in the ground for an extra twenty minutes after everybody else had been let out while they decided what to do with us. As we stood and waited, we could see a load of Frontline lads from our vantage point at the top of the stand so we filled a couple of socks with loose change to create a set of makeshift weapons. We were badly outnumbered and it looked as if we were going to have a battle on our hands.

The coppers had promised that we were going to get an escort to our van but then changed their minds. As soon as we got through the stiles they told us to fuck off. They obviously couldn't be arsed taking us the full way, which left us having to contend with the swarm of angry Middlesbrough lads that had gathered outside the stadium. We swung our loaded socks at them and managed to get past but there were fucking tons of them and they legged us up the road towards the park, looking to do us some mischief. Lucky for us a load of Old Bill turned up in cars and kept the Boro lads near the ground while we got into our van. As the coppers escorted us out of Middlesbrough, we mopped our brows and breathed a collective sigh of relief. It had been a proper close call and we were happy to have made it out of there in one piece.

Rather than heading straight back home to Bolton, we stopped off in a place called Thornaby, which is near Stockton, so that we could top up on beer and get something to eat. A couple of the lads went to the chippie and the rest of us went to the off licence to get some more cans. The group I was with robbed the offy blind and we were loading our ill-gotten gains into the van when we noticed a load of casually dressed lads, going at it with the rest of our firm outside the chippie. They were from Blyth in Northumberland but they were Middlesbrough lads and they were intent on giving us a second chance.

We went running over to help our mates and, before I knew it, it was going off big style. It was proper toe to toe and neither side was backing off. Part way into the fight, the Old Bill arrived on the scene and fucked us off to our van in typical killjoy fashion. I was surprised that nobody ended up getting nicked, as the coppers would usually want to haul us down to the station for a disturbance on that scale. I think we rode our luck a bit. Still, we didn't want to push things so we set off on the long drive home, keeping ourselves entertained by drinking and playing cards along the way. We'd had our fair share of action and it was time to call it a day.

The Frontline are definitely a game set of lads and they provided us with some stiff competition. It was neck and neck with the boys from Blyth but that hasn't always been the case when Bolton have played Boro, as we've run a few of their lads about the place over the years. Our home game against them in November 1987 springs to mind. Forty of us met up in Space City on the day of the match, ready to do battle. The atmosphere in the bar was fairly relaxed, which was strange considering what a formidable opponent we were about to face. We were laughing and joking and reminiscing back to the time when a lad called Nick had tried to cut the CCTV cables in Burnden Park. Luckily for him he wasn't successful, as he would have probably electrocuted himself but it provided us with an endless source of amusement.

We were sat there pondering what had possessed Nick to put his life on the line for the sake of a couple of cameras when some lads from Little Lever came running into the bar with a look of nervous excitement plastered across their faces.

'We've just had a row with Boro,' one of them breathlessly exclaimed. 'The Old Bill came and broke it up. I reckon we would have got a hiding if they hadn't have turned up.'

'Game on,' I thought.

We downed our pints and headed into the centre to look for our rivals but they were nowhere to be seen so we plotted up in the King William on Bradshawgate and got a couple more drinks in. At half one, the word got round that Boro were drinking at the Sweet Green Tavern on Crook Street so we armed ourselves with bottles and pool cues and set off to do battle. As it turned out, we didn't even have to bother going to their boozer to get a fight, because we saw between thirty and forty of their lads walking down the street and ran straight into them, scattering them all over the place. We caught up with a few and left them in a pretty nasty state.

Buzzing about our first victory of the day, we headed on to the Sweet Green and saw a couple of Frontline lads outside. We ran them into the pub and smashed the windows of the boozer and they retaliated by throwing tables and chairs back out at us. This went on for a good ten minutes until the Old Bill turned up in force to put a stop to things. The coppers charged into us, nicking anybody they could get their hands on and hitting us with their batons. The mounted police ended up chasing us through Bolton town centre as the pedestrian officers escorted Middlesbrough's firm to the ground. Once again, the Old Bill had put an end to our fun and prevented us from doing our rivals over.

Shortly after we had managed to shake the coppers off, we made our way to the ground, disappointed that we weren't going to get another row in before the match. The game itself was fairly uneventful. There were a couple of isolated incidents but nothing to write home about.

We lost 1–0 and there were hordes of Bolton lads waiting around outside the ground for Middlesbrough after the final whistle had blown. It would have gone off proper if the coppers hadn't kept our opponents in for an extra thirty minutes to prevent any more disturbances.

Although we were denied the opportunity to have another ruck with the Frontline, it was still well worthwhile going to the game, as we demonstrated that we could hold our own against one of the best firms in the country. Boro were a class outfit and by doing well against them, we showed that we could compete with the crème de la crème. Overall I would say that we upheld the pride of our team and put in an impressive performance against a decent bunch of lads.

14

PORTSMOUTH

Pompey are definitely one of the best southern mobs. The Old Bill have branded them 'the worst in Britain' and while I don't necessarily agree with that assessment, they are certainly up there with the main contenders. Their 6.57 Crew are generally regarded as one of the most active firms in the country and when I heard that we were playing them in May 2005, I was proper made up. They had been involved in several high-profile incidents – including a riot in which ninety-three people were arrested in March 2004 – and if their reputation was anything to go by we would have our work cut out.

On the day of the match, a hundred-plus Cuckoo Boys met up at a pub in Bolton town centre at five o'clock in the morning, ready to make the journey down south. It was mainly our older firm but there were also a fair few younger lads with us and we were well stocked up with drink and drugs, the essential ingredients for a long coach trip.

During the journey, I kept the rest of the firm entertained by blasting them with a little toy gun that fired miniature plastic balls. I must have shot at least three-quarters of our boys in the back of the neck by the time we got to Portsmouth, which seemed to piss a fair few people off. We arrived in Pompey just after twelve and we were straight into the pubs to get our fill of beer before the game kicked off. There were seven or eight 6.57 lads in the boozer but nobody bothered them because there were only a handful of them and there was a massive mob of us.

Some of the lads didn't have any tickets so at twenty to three, nine of us set off to find a pub that had a telly so that we could watch the game. The boozer that we chose had a couple of 6.57 in it and they immediately started mouthing off and giving us shit.

'Come on then,' one of our lot shouted over to them. 'Let's 'ave it.'

The Pompey lads started issuing threats of their own and we were involved in a bit of a stand off with them, with neither firm wanting to be the first to throw a punch. One of the Farnworth lot eventually flared it off and the entire pub descended into chaos. Tables, chairs, glasses and bottles flew around the place and a Farnworth lad got hit in the back of the neck with an ashtray. He was cut up pretty badly but Pompey showed no mercy. There seemed to be more and more of them every time I looked and they were all game.

After a couple of minutes of going at it, I realised where the extra 6.57 lads had come from. Somebody had opened the fire exit and they had snuck in through there. We were badly outnumbered and the bird behind the bar had decided to help our rivals by pelting us with ashtrays. The pub was soon too packed for us to move and just to make matters worse, some cunt decided to launch a table across the room, knocking me onto my arse. I got a couple of boots to the head while I was on the floor but luckily one of my mates was on hand to pull me up and I was straight back into the fray, punching and kicking for all I was worth.

After a good few minutes of fighting, the Old Bill arrived on the scene and one of them grabbed hold of me and hauled me out of the building. At first I thought he was going to nick me but he was mainly concerned with splitting up the warring sets of hooligans. He was content with removing me from the pub so that I couldn't carry on scrapping. The canine units weren't quite as merciful and one of our lads got chewed up pretty badly. He was in a right state and I think the plod were well out of order for letting him get bitten to pieces like that.

The Old Bill eventually managed to form a line in front of us and our rivals passively stood behind it, failing to make any effort to get at us. The coppers started swinging their batons at us and pushing us down the road. Most of them were on foot but a handful were on mountain bikes. I had never seen Old Bill on mountain bikes before and it took me completely by surprise.

PORTSMOUTH

After a brief struggle, the OB rounded us up and walked us to the ground so that we couldn't get up to any more shenanigans before the game kicked off. They took us past a load of Pompey lads who were queuing up to get inside the stadium and, to their credit, a few of them tried to jump into the escort and have it with us. They ended up getting either slapped or nicked but, fair play to them, they were a crazy set of bastards and they were a lot gamer than the boys at the pub. They were determined to have it with us, Old Bill or no Old Bill, and they didn't mind risking their freedom in the process.

The game was a 1–1 draw and as soon as it had finished, the coppers were back on our case, pushing us down the road towards the coaches. Some of the lads managed to slip away and get back into the pubs but the majority of us were herded through the town like a flock of sheep until we reached our vehicles.

'Right, ring the rest of your lads up,' one of the coppers told me once we had got to our coach. 'You've got ten minutes to get everybody here. You're getting out of Portsmouth.'

They couldn't wait to get rid of us. I got the impression that they were still pissed off about our antics before the game.

As soon as we had the entire firm on board, the coach headed off, back to Bolton. The driver was a proper sound bloke and parked up outside a Tesco part way through the journey so that we could buy some more beers. His opinion of us didn't seem to have been swayed by the attitude of the Pompey Old Bill. He even allowed us to stop off for an hour to break up our return trip.

Shortly after we arrived home, we headed off to the Ikon nightclub in Bolton town centre. Even the fella who had been hit with the ashtray came along. He cleaned himself up, borrowed a jumper and carried on as if nothing had happened. What a lad!

Portsmouth were a decent firm but we definitely held our own. It just goes to show you that if you're willing to stand your ground, you can take on a tasty mob with superior numbers at their disposal and still do okay.

15

BLACKPOOL

The amount of lads that a firm has got with them isn't always the defining factor when it comes to predicting how well they are going to do. You can have the biggest mob in the world but if none of them are willing to stand then you are destined for failure. The same is true of the individual fighting skills of the lads in your firm. You can all be as hard as fuck but if you are unwilling to give it your all then you are going to have a struggle on your hands.

Whereas the majority of firms that we came up against were driven by their desire to enhance their reputations, there was one mob that was motivated solely by revenge. They weren't the largest mob, and they weren't the hardest either, but they hated Bolton with a passion and they were willing to do whatever it took to hurt us.

Our rivalry with Blackpool started in August 1974 when a seventeen-year-old Blackpool fan was stabbed to death at the back of the Spion Kop during a game against Bolton. He died shortly afterwards and his murder was described by a *Match of the Day* commentator as, 'the ultimate outrage of senseless football gang war and hooliganism'. The Blackpool lads were furious and they vowed never to let it lie. And rightly so. Nobody expects to lose their life at the football and it should never have been allowed to happen. One of our older lads remembers the game in question only too well . . .

Older lad

I was only fifteen at the time and, to be honest, I only looked about twelve. I was a skinny, inexperienced teenager and I have to admit that I was more than a little apprehensive about going to the game. I knew which other lads were going and I had no doubt in my mind that they were going to cause complete and utter carnage.

Most of the lads who got the train down to Blackpool that morning were in their late twenties and early thirties and I can remember feeling that I was a child among adults. Still, I felt safe with them, as I knew that they would have my back covered if anything went off. They were excitedly chattering away, talking about their previous battles, and I was lapping up their stories, wishing that I had some more of my own to tell. A lot of them were skins and they all had black Crombies, white skinners and Doc Martin boots on. They had a real sense of purpose, as if they were heroic soldiers planning a mission behind enemy lines.

We got the ten o'clock train, arriving in Blackpool just after half eleven and, fortunately, there were only a handful of Old Bill waiting for us at the platform. We were able to brush past them fairly easily and the minute we set foot outside, all of our older lads started rampaging through the town. They smashed up shops and pubs and stole anything they could get their hands on.

The coppers weren't best pleased about the trail of devastation that we were leaving and they were soon batoning people about the place, attempting to regain control of the streets. Some of the Bolton lads retaliated by throwing bricks at their horses and kicking their dogs and a couple of our boys got nicked. Blackpool didn't have what I would call a proper mob out. It was mainly smaller groups of lads, doing their best to avoid us. They were dealt with pretty quickly and none of them were able to put up much resistance.

After a couple of hours of bowling around the town, smashing windows and chasing rival lads, the coppers turned out in force and we were escorted to the ground. As a final precaution to prevent us from causing any more trouble inside the stadium, our entire firm was searched before we were allowed in. Knives were dropped onto the floor right, left and centre and one lad got arrested for trying to sneak a pair of knuckledusters through the turnstiles.

The atmosphere inside the ground was tense as fuck. Missiles were flying about the place and there were fights breaking out all over the stadium. I was excited by the danger. It was like rival sets of gladiators, battling it out in an arena. Lads were getting hauled out by the Old Bill every couple of minutes and it felt as if anything could go off at any given moment.

By the time it got to half-time, the action had reached fever pitch and both mobs were gathered at the kiosk at the bottom of the steps, looking to cause each other some serious harm. After a brief confrontation, Bolton managed to back Blackpool off into their side of the Kop but then, in the midst of all the carnage, one of our lot pulled out a knife and stuck it into a young lad's back. I didn't see it happen but from what I have read about it in the papers, the victim was unarmed and he had very little chance of defending himself. Seventeen-year-old Kevin Olsson later died from his injuries.

'There has been a fatality,' came a voice over the tannoy. 'Bolton fans will be kept in once the match has finished so that they can provide the police with their details and volunteer any information that they might have.'

My heart skipped a beat. I felt sick inside and a wave of shock washed over me. It was crazy to think that somebody could go to watch a football match and end up losing his life.

Whereas some of our fans were visibly upset by what had happened, others were laughing and joking. They were singing, 'We are the only team to kill a Blackpool fan.' The Blackpool supporters looked fucking furious. They were pelting us with projectiles and scowling at us across the terraces. I was worried about what might happen to us once the final whistle had blown.

We were kept back for a full hour after the game had finished so that the Old Bill could I.D. us and take our details. This gave Blackpool's firm some extra time to mob up. By this stage, they were looking to fucking murder us. We were eventually allowed to leave the ground in groups of ones and twos and the minute we got outside they were on us. Dribs and drabs of Bolton supporters got the shit kicked out of them all the way back to the station and some of our lads ended up getting pretty badly hurt. I was fortunate enough to be placed in a police escort, which was probably the only thing that prevented me from getting my head kicked in. It wasn't just Blackpool's hooligans that were out to get us; their regular fans were baying for our blood as well. They were devastated by what had happened to their fellow Seasider and they were determined to take their revenge.

I didn't go to any more football matches for a while after that, as the killing had left a nasty taste in my mouth. Nobody was ever convicted, although we had a fair idea of who did it and the main suspect got beaten up and driven out of town. We aren't heartless and we've all got emotions. Kevin Olsson had a family and his parents were deprived of their son over a game of football. It was a tragic incident and one that we all deeply regret.

'ONE might say Blackpool and Bolton have history,' wrote a reporter for the Blackpool Gazette in November 2010. 'Most of it is good. There have been some fabulous footballing encounters between the Lancashire clubs over the years, the best at Wembley in 1953, when two Stanleys famously combined to swing events in the Seasiders' favour. There has been one awful, bleak moment though. August 1974, when 17-year-old Blackpool supporter Kevin Olsson was stabbed on the terraces at Bloomfield Road during a game. . . . But it is important to remember that one random act of terrible violence isn't a true reflection of the relationship between Blackpool and Bolton. The clubs have met 91 times (and on 18 occasions since Kevin's death) and the majority have passed without incident.'

The fact that the killing is still being talked about thirty-six years after it took place is testament to the level of hatred it evoked within the Blackpool support. The majority of games we have played against them have certainly not been incident-free, despite the efforts of the media to make out that the rivalry between the two clubs is a thing of the past. Blackpool's Muckers firm are never going to forget about the death of a seventeen-year-old lad and our matches against them will forever be fraught with danger. They hate us with a passion and turn out in force whenever we meet.

Considering the fact that the Blackpool fans are still out to get us, you can imagine how tense the situation was when we played them again, at home, two months after Kevin's death. As far as they were concerned, we were a load of murdering bastards who deserved to die. It was a scary match to go to but, then again, those were always the most exciting games to attend and now that Blackpool's mob were intent on having their revenge, we were guaranteed to get a fight.

We arrived in Bolton town centre at one in the afternoon. Me and my mates were all too young to drink so we couldn't go into any of the pubs. We ended up traipsing around the place instead, hoping to bump into some of Blackpool's mob but, strangely enough, there weren't all that many of them about. There were plenty of Old Bill patrolling the streets but they didn't seem to have anybody to police, as there was no sign of any trouble.

By the time it got to two o'clock, we were beginning to worry that it was going to be a relatively peaceful game. We had just bought ourselves some chips and peas to eat and we were stuffing ourselves full of them when we saw a load of coppers running down towards the station, alerting us to the fact that *something was about to go off. Sure enough, a group of menacing-looking Blackpool lads came bowling out of the entrance, chanting, 'Seasiders! Seasiders!' There were around fifty of them and some of them were fucking huge.*

The Bolton boys immediately started piling out of the nearby pubs. Our lads were proper raring to do battle but no matter how hard they tried they couldn't get past the plod. A hundred-and-fifty-strong mob of Bolton ended up following the Seasiders all the way to the ground, looking to do them in. The Old Bill were really on the ball that day and they managed to shepherd both mobs into the ground without so much as a single punch being thrown. They had their horses and their dogs there and it was impossible to get around them.

I made my way into the Lever End, disappointed that the coppers had ruined our fun, and I was surprised to see between eighty and ninety Seasiders standing near the fence. The cheeky fucking bastards! Within minutes, all hell had broken loose and a hefty mob of Bolton was running down the terraces with fists and feet flying. How dare they attempt to gain a foothold in our end.

A rousing chant of 'Bolton aggro' permeated round the stadium and the two rival firms started going at it tooth and nail. Blackpool did well to start off with but we managed to back them off onto the pitch and a couple of them ended up with ripped shirts and bloody faces. There were far too many of our lads there for them to stand a chance and they got badly leathered. The Old Bill arrived at the scene fairly quickly and the Blackpool lads were escorted back round the pitch to the Embankment End, where they were applauded by their fans. Fair play to them, they made their point and they were brave for coming into the Lever. It was the only time they ever ventured into our home end and it showed they had balls.

There were a few minor scuffles in the Embankment during the game but nothing particularly impressive went off, despite the fact that we had over a hundred of our lads in their end. I guess that all of the gamest members of their firm must have been in the Lever.

After the match had finished, a couple of hundred Boltonians decided to lay in wait for Blackpool's mob outside the ground. We would have fucking leathered them if the Old Bill hadn't kept them in for twenty extra minutes after the final whistle had blown. By the time our rivals were allowed out, the coppers had managed to clear our lads away, ready to escort their firm to the station.

Blackpool may not be one of the main contenders when it comes to football hooliganism but, when they are playing us, they pull out all the stops. Saying that though, being 100 per cent honest, they have never managed to do that much, despite the levels of animosity they've got for us, and I still don't rate them very highly. Fair enough they went in our end but we had lads in their end too. They are not one of the worst mobs by any means but they aren't anything special either and they need to do a damn sight better if they want to come out on top against us.

The hatred that Blackpool harboured towards us all those years ago continued well into the Eighties and Nineties. It is difficult to forget the death of a young lad and they had good reason to continue the grudge. We had an equally heated battle with them on 18 April 1989 when we played them in the Sherpa Van Trophy tournament. Whereas most teams classed the Sherpa as a bit of a Mickey Mouse cup, it was an important match for us, because if we won the game we would get to play at Wembley for the first time since 1958, when we beat the Scum 2-0 in the FA Cup final. We had sold our entire allocation of 4,500 tickets and the word was going round that an equal number of lads were going to make their way there without briefs. We were going to have an impressive turnout.

On the day of the match, fifteen of us travelled down in a van and arrived in Blackpool at 6.30 p.m. We parked up at a side street about a mile away from the ground and made our way to the game, hoping that we'd bump into some more of our firm along the way. Part way through the journey we saw another group of Bolton lads walking along the street and asked them if they had had any trouble off the Blackpool lot yet.

'We've had a few small offs,' one of them told me. 'Nothing major though.'

Oh well, I thought, we'll have plenty of time for that later on.

When we arrived at the ground, there was a long queue outside the turnstiles so a load of us walked around the stadium to try and get into Blackpool's end. The minute we got within a couple of hundred yards of it, our opponents were onto us and they started up their usual shitty chants of, 'Seasiders, Seasiders'. This alerted the Old Bill to our presence and they charged straight into us with their batons, much to the amusement of the Blackpool fans. We were eventually made to go into a packed side paddock where there was barely enough room to breathe.

Because there were so many of us crowded into the same section of the ground a couple of hundred Bolton lads clambered over a fence and into an empty terrace on the right hand side of the Spion Kop. It was decrepit and looked as if it hadn't been used in ages. The Old Bill didn't seem to mind us occupying the abandoned section of the stadium, as the enclosure that they had put us in was clearly rammed to capacity. However, all that changed when thirty Blackpool fans climbed over from the opposite paddock just after kickoff and started giving us verbals. We retaliated by throwing pieces of concrete at them and the coppers hurried into our section with their batons drawn, intent on putting a stop to the trouble before it got any worse. We soon calmed down and we were left to watch the rest of the match without any further hassle.

We won the game 1–0, which sparked a miniature pitch invasion by our fans. Some of Blackpool's lads ran onto the grass to confront them but we weren't having any of it and a load more Bolton supporters jumped the fences and ran them back into their end. They were climbing the fences as if their lives depended upon it.

Outside the ground, mobs of Bolton lads were celebrating our victory all over the town. Nothing was really kicking off with the Seasiders but I wasn't that bothered, as I was proper made up at the prospect of playing at Wembley. I didn't care that the Sherpa Van Trophy was supposedly a Mickey Mouse cup. We had still got a result and we had managed to turn the Muckers over on their own ground.

Blackpool have definitely got a couple of game lads but they aren't anything special. Credit where it's due, they tried their luck with us in the stadium but they will have to do a lot better than that if they want to get a result. You would have thought that a firm that hate us as much as they do would be able to do a lot more damage but I am still waiting for the day that they take us. Until it arrives, we will continue to run them around the place and they will carry on getting done in on their own patch.

16
BLACKBURN

Although Blackpool have their flaws, they are still nowhere near as pitiful as one of the other main Lancashire firms, the consistently hopeless Blackburn Casuals crew. Blackburn very rarely turn out for us and, when they do, they nearly always end up on their toes.

Football hooliganism isn't about being hard, it's about being game. You could have the softest set of lads in the world but if they are willing to stand and fight against the hardest set of lads they immediately gain my respect. The problem with Blackburn is that they don't even try. We have been running them ragged for a good thirty years now. Here's one of our seasoned veterans to tell you about our run-in with them in April 1978 . . .

Older lad

I was looking forward to giving Blackburn's firm a good kicking, as I've always hated them ever since I got nicked for violence at their ground in 1973. I was only fifteen at the time and it left a nasty taste in my mouth, resulting in me classing Blackburn versus Bolton as a proper grudge match. This particular game would be even more intense than usual, as we needed to win to gain promotion to the old first division and we were expecting up to eighteen thousand of our fans to be in attendance. Both the football and the violence were looking set to be exciting as fuck.

On the day of the match, thirty of us set off early from Farnworth, eager to get a row in before the game kicked off. When we got to Blackburn there were only a handful of Old Bill about so we went straight into their mob's main boozer, the Adelphi pub, which is opposite the station. It was packed with our lads and our rivals were nowhere to be seen. We stayed for a couple of drinks and then we went for a wander around the town to see if we could find their firm.

We didn't see any of Blackburn's lads but we saw plenty of looted shops and a bar that had been wrecked, which was a sign that the rest of our firm had been working their magic. We decided to keep a fairly low profile, as we knew that Bolton's thieving spree would attract a fair few Old Bill to the scene. It is always best to avoid getting nicked before you've even entered the ground, if you can possibly help it. Rather than continuing to look for our opponents, we piled into a quiet little bar down one of the side streets, where we ordered ourselves a couple more beers and sat about sipping our pints. By the time we finally started making our way to the ground, the rest of our firm were out in force.

'The Old Bill are going to have their work cut out tonight,' I remarked to a lad called Craig. 'We've got enough lads with us and they're all pissed up. I wouldn't like to have to do the coppers' job after the match has finished.'

There were a couple of regular Blackburn fans scattered around the place but their hooligans were nowhere to be seen. We managed to make our way into their end completely unopposed and stood near the back of the paddock, keeping our eyes peeled for any sign of trouble. We quickly spotted Blackburn's firm. They must have snuck into the stadium in ones and twos to avoid us getting onto them. We were going to make them pay for refusing to show their faces prior to the game.

Within a split second, a horde of Bolton lads had surged forward into Blackburn's mob and a rousing chant of 'Bolton aggro' was echoing round the terraces. We kicked and punched our rivals from every direction and they panicked like fuck, desperately attempting to get away. They ended up running out onto the pitch and a few of our lads chased them onto the grass, where we were finally able to give them the beating they deserved.

After a good couple of minutes of us kicking Blackburn's heads in, the Old Bill managed to get the situation under control and we settled down to watch the game. For once the football was on a par with the violence and we won 1–0, with Frank Worthington scoring the goal. The minute the final whistle had blown, thousands of Bolton supporters invaded the pitch from every section of the ground. We had just won promotion to the first division. It was the ultimate victory and I was as chuffed as fuck.

Most of Blackburn's lads had left the ground before the end of the game and the remainder slunk off unnoticed into the darkness to lick their wounds. They must have been devastated. We had humiliated them on and off the pitch and out of a gate of 27,000, nearly 20,000 of the attendees were Bolton supporters. We had taken over their town, taken over their stadium and beaten their team. What more could we have asked for? If they had stood their ground against us they would have at least had that to be proud of but they did fuck all. We took the fucking piss and they stood meekly by and allowed us to do it.

I have been involved in a number of battles with Blackburn over the years and most times we've come up against them, they have either totally avoided us or run away at the first sign of trouble. Saying that though, every team has got a handful of decent lads with them, no matter how shit they are, and there have been a couple of occasions when they have managed to put up a fight. They battered a fair few of our lads during a game at Burnden Park in December 1989. It was funny because I had caught the bus straight to the ground, as I didn't think that there would be any chance of them bringing a firm along. Then, lo and behold, I saw a load of their lads laying into our scarfers on the way to the game. I was surprised, as I never usually see hide nor hair of them until the match. At the same time, however, I was deeply angered by their actions, as they were picking on people who didn't want to know. It was time to teach the cunts a lesson.

I got off the bus just outside the car park and walked straight across to the away end to give Blackburn's firm a piece of my mind. The rest of our mob had decided to do the same and a horde of angry Bolton lads were gathered around the stiles, yelling threats and insults at our rivals. We were pissed off that they had taken advantage of our fans like that and wanted to let them know that we were gunning for them.

Blackburn were hurling abuse back over at us and this fat ginger cunt at the front was being particularly mouthy. I can remember thinking, 'Right you lardy fucker, I'm going to have you.' Gingers are a pain in the arse at the best of times but when they're giving you the verbals like that, they are even worse than usual. I started giving the wanker sign to the ginger and a copper came across and gave me a bollocking for it, telling me that he was going to nick me if I didn't calm down. I wanted to ask him where the fuck he was when Blackburn were battering our shirters but I kept my mouth shut. It was easier to toe the line so I went inside the stadium and left my redheaded friend to carry on giving it the big one.

Blackburn had virtually filled the away end by the time I got into the ground. They were in high spirits, singing, 'Wanky wanky Wanderers' and chanting abuse at us. If they had known that a small mob of our lads had managed to make it right into the middle of their end they might have kept their mouths shut but, as it was, they were blissfully unaware. We would see how well they fared when they were faced with a set of our hooligans, rather than our shirters.

Shortly after the players had walked out onto the pitch, twenty to thirty of our boys broke out into a Bolton song, alerting our opponents to the presence of a group of rival lads in their midst. A gap appeared around our lads and there was a moment's hesitation as Blackburn decided what they were going to do. They seemed a little apprehensive at first but when they realised how badly outnumbered we were, they were straight into our mob, swarming all over them like a cloud of angry wasps.

There were far too many Blackburn lads for our boys to contend with and some of them ended up getting kicked to fuck on the floor. We were trying to climb over the fences to get into the away end and help them out, but, by this stage, the Old Bill were batoning all and sundry and it was impossible to reach them. 'Bolton aggro!' roared our fans. 'Bolton aggro!' It was all very well chanting words of encouragement over to our lads but it was going to take a damn sight more than that to save them. They were getting fucking hammered and, for once, Blackburn were actually doing something against us.

Eventually, the police dogs arrived on the scene and a group of blood-stained Bolton lads were dragged out of Blackburn's end, looking considerably worse for wear. Some of them had got a right good pasting and I think they must have been relieved that the coppers had intervened. Our opponents had done well against a small section of our firm but they still had to face the bulk of our mob once they got outside. We would see if they could repeat the performance when they were faced with equal numbers. We were still pissed off about what they had done to our shirters and the fact that they had managed to get one over on us in the ground only added fuel to the flames.

We drew 2–2 in the end and that fat ginger cunt wound us up from across *the pitch for the entire ninety minutes. It got to the point where we couldn't wait to get outside the ground so that we could do him in. As soon as the final whistle had blown, a couple of hundred Bolton lads positioned themselves on Manchester Road ready for revenge. It was time to even the score.*

As soon as Blackburn's firm reached the Manny Road, we charged down the street towards them and the vast majority of them were immediately on their toes. They had done more than they usually did against us but they were still unwilling to have it with our full mob and even the ginger twat was legging it, which was pretty funny given the amount of mouthing off he had been doing.

'Where the fuck do you think you're going?' I shouted, bemused that somebody with that much of a gob on them was such a fucking coward. 'Get back here, you ginger bastard.'

Luckily the ginger gobshite was fairly slow at running on account of being such a fat cunt and I was able to catch up with him relatively quickly. I got a grip of him on the side of a large grass verge and I can remember thinking, 'This is the moment I've been waiting for all day long.' I was just getting stuck into him when I saw a sudden flash of blue and the next thing I knew, a pair of coppers were hitting me in the face and pushing me onto the floor.

'You fucking killjoys,' I thought to myself, 'Now that ginger wanker is going to get away.'

'We're charging you with breach of the peace,' one of the Old Bill told me as he shoved me into the back of a police van, ready to cart me off to Bolton Central police station on Scholey Street, just off Manny Road. 'You do not have to say anything but anything that you do say may be used in evidence against you in a court of law.'

Fuck! Now I was going to miss out on the action.

It was ten at night by the time I was released and I headed straight back into Bolton town centre to find out what had happened after I had been nicked.

'Blackburn got turned over good and proper,' one of my mates filled me in. 'That fat, ginger-haired lad got arrested too just after the coppers got you.'

Result! The fact that I had spent the day in the cells suddenly didn't seem as bad now that I knew my archrival had suffered the same fate.

'Blackburn fractured a shirter's eye socket before the game,' another lad told me. 'They were jumping up and down on his face.'

The dirty bastards. We should have battered them a lot more than we did but at least we had got some kind of revenge. I guess if you've got as shit a mob as Blackburn then your only hope of coming out on top is to pick a fight with a bunch of non-violent shirters or victimise a smaller groups of lads. That was what they did fifteen years down the line in February 1996, proving that a leopard can never change its spots. Phil was there to witness it and it cost him a £180 fine, a night in the cells and an exclusion order, although he remains adamant that it was still worthwhile . . .

Phil

Blackburn is one of those towns that we take over every time we go there. It's only a half-hour train journey from Bolton and we turn out in force whenever we're playing them. Even the lads who don't turn up every week can be guaranteed to be at Blackburn because it is such a tasty day out. A fair few of the local boozers usually end up getting smashed and by the time we head home, we have usually left their town centre looking like a bomb's gone off.

This particular day was no exception and the train was packed with the usual faces. There were a good two hundred of our lads on board. My brother Stewart and I spent the entire journey down there drinking Thunderbird and getting pissed, which made it a more enjoyable half hour and got us fired up for a fight.

Sixty of us decided to leave the train at Darwen, as we thought we would get less hassle off the Old Bill there. We split up into smaller groups, making sure that we were never more than a single pub behind each other. We gradually worked our way through all the local boozers until we got to Blackburn, where we headed off to the ground, buzzing in anticipation of going in their end.

Infiltrating another team's seats always adds to the excitement. It guarantees you a fight and it is a way of proving how game you are. We divided ourselves up into groups of ten and positioned ourselves around the home end, ready to fly into our rivals as soon as they cottoned on to us. I was stood with a load of other lads from Little Lever and I could see hooligans from various other areas of Bolton dotted around the stand. There must have been six hundred of our lads in the home end and I could hardly wait for our opponents to realise that we were there. They were going to have a right battle on their hands.

The match kicked off and before I knew it, they were beating us 2–1.

'Fuck this,' I said to my brother, 'If they score again, I'm kicking it off.'

Sure enough, twenty minutes before the end of the game, Alan Shearer banged one in and the crowd around us got up on their feet to celebrate.

'Not yet,' Stewart insisted, pushing me back down into my seat as I rose up to get at the Blackburn fans. 'Just calm down. We'll have our chance to get into them later on.'

As I was contemplating whether or not to take my brother's advice, a big skinhead lad started gesticulating at one of my mates, giving him the wanker sign and leaving me with no doubt as to what I had to do. My mate was a kick boxer and he could definitely handle himself but, for whatever reason, he was standing there doing nothing so I clambered over the seats and kicked things off on his behalf.

I butted the skinhead in his face and the next thing I knew, we were brawling away between the seats, beating the living daylights out of one another. I was just getting stuck into him when a steward grabbed hold of me from behind and flung me down a stairwell by my neck. I was now in full attack mode and nothing could prevent me from going at it. Adrenalin was pumping through my body at a million miles per hour and I was proper itching to do some damage.

By the time I had gathered myself up from off the floor, every man and his dog was fighting and the stadium had descended into an all-out riot. I started to make my way down the stairs to join in with the action only to be confronted by a crazy-looking Blackburn lad holding . . . was it a knife? No, not a knife. It was a fucking surgical scalpel!

'Come on then, you Bolton bastards,' yelled Scalpel Man. 'I'll fucking cut you.'

I have to admit, he stopped me dead in my tracks. You can't go around tackling people with blades and expect to walk away in one piece and I didn't want to end up getting hacked to death by the cunt. I was stood there trying to work out what the best way of dealing with him would be when one of our lads came running in from behind and twatted him to the ground. Well, that was one way of resolving the situation. Now if I could only avoid the monstrous amounts of Old Bill that had descended upon the terraces I'd be sorted. I managed to make it over to the area where they were selling the pies and I was just stopping to contemplate the sheer insanity of Scalpel Man when three rival hooligans came bowling over, looking to start a ruck.

'You're fucking having it,' one of them snarled.

Luckily, a couple of other Bolton lads were on hand to even up the score and a lad called Mike was straight into them, smacking them about the place with ease and effortlessly breaking their resolve. Within a couple of minutes of it kicking off, we'd got them on their toes and they were legging it across the stadium, fearing for their lives. Once we had grown tired of chasing our opponents about the place, we decided to make our way down the steps to the ground floor to join in with what was going on there. We were halfway down the stairs when a group of Old Bill came running across the terraces to arrest us.

It was just my fucking luck.

The coppers slapped the cuffs onto us before we had a chance to get away and I can remember thinking, 'Shit, my missus is going to kill me.' I was supposed to be taking her for a meal that night and she wasn't going to be pleased when she found out that I would be spending the evening at the cop shop instead. As we were herded into the back of the police van, I could hear the roar of angry football hooligans in the distance and I felt disappointed that I wasn't going to get to stay and fight. Typical Old Bill, always ruining our fun.

When we got to the station, the coppers threw us into a cell and a senior officer came to break the news that I was the only one that was getting charged. 'There's clear footage of you fighting on the CCTV,' he told me. 'I've got to compliment you on your fighting skills but there's no getting out of this one. We've got you bang to rights.'

We were kept in the cells until half eight at night to prevent us from causing any more trouble with Blackburn. Then the desk sergeant provided me with my charge sheet and my court date and issued me with a few words of warning.

'Go straight to the train station,' he told me. 'All of your boys have gone home and there are a lot of Blackburn supporters around.'

By this stage, the streets were full of people on nights out and I was left wandering around like a headless chicken, worse for wear after the punches that I'd taken at the ground and looking decidedly out of place among the carefree weekend revellers.

'Excuse me love.' My only hope of making it back home in one piece was to ask a random passer-by where I was going. 'Do you know what the quickest way to the station is?'

Luckily, the woman that I approached was able to give me directions and I stumbled on through the streets, hoping that I could successfully complete my journey before any Blackburn lads got onto me.

As I approached the street that the station was on, I noticed there were a lot of police cars darting around. Time to lace my boots up, I thought to myself. The Old Bill had taken my shoelaces out in case I tried to hang myself with them in the cells and I hadn't bothered to replace them. There was almost certainly something going off and I didn't want my shoes to come flying off if I needed to do a runner.

The minute I turned the corner at the end of the street, I was confronted by what could have easily passed for a war zone. Glasses were flying about the place and people were hitting each other with scaffolding poles right, left and centre. There was also an immense amount of Old Bill on the scene so I decided to make my way around the mêlée to where a couple of lads that I knew were standing, as there was no point in getting involved in the fighting in full view of the coppers. I didn't want them to haul my arse straight back down to the station.

The Old Bill eventually managed to herd the Blackburn lads down the street, away from the Bolton lot. We had a mooch round a couple of the nearby boozers to see if any of them had gone inside but they were nowhere to be seen so we decided to get a couple of drinks down us instead. There was still a full hour and ten minutes to kill before our train arrived and I figured that we might as well spend it getting pissed.

Eight of us headed down a little ginnel at the side of the station and went into one of the boozers round there. It seemed as good a place as any to sit and sup our beers and, by this stage, we were resigned to the fact that we weren't going to get another fight in before we had to leave.

'Where do you think the rest of the lads have got to?' I asked my mate, as we sat around a table drinking our pints.

There had been a good thirty Cuckoo Boys stood around near the station and I had assumed they would be joining us.

'I don't know,' he replied. 'I wonder where they've gone . . .'

The words had barely left his mouth when both pub doors flew open and a set of casually dressed lads came storming in.

'Well these lot certainly aren't from Bolton,' I said. 'It looks like we're going to get another fight in after all.'

It was typical of Blackburn to pick off the stragglers while the rest of our mob were God knows where. They will only ever take on groups of twenty or less.

Our rivals didn't waste time in kicking things off. This big, bald fucker bowled straight across to where we were sitting and started mouthing off at a lad called Nick. While he was running his gums, his mates positioned themselves nearby, ready to jump in. There were forty of them and eight of us and I knew full well that we were going to get our arses kicked. Sure enough, after a couple of minutes of threatening us, the bald guy raised both of his hands above his head and two-hand smashed Nick onto the floor, knocking him clean out.

'Shit,' I thought to myself, 'We've really fucked it here. They're going to fucking slaughter us.'

Within the space of a split second, another of our lads had beaten the bald cunt unconscious with a bottle and we were going at it hammer and tongs with Blackburn's firm. They had us boxed into the corner of the boozer and there was nowhere for us to run. We would have to stand and fight, regardless of the odds.

In an effort to prevent ourselves from getting killed, we turned a table on its side and crouched down behind it, using it as a makeshift shield as we pelted our rivals with bottles and ornamental plant pots. Blackburn responded by hurling anything that they could get their hands on back across the pub. They were throwing chairs, tables, bricks, you name it.

After a good few minutes of going at it, we decided that we were going to end up getting ourselves hospitalised if we stayed around any longer so we armed ourselves with bottles and made a run for the door. As I went past Blackburn's lads, I felt a volley of bottles, fists and feet connecting with my head and body. If I made it back home in one piece it would be a fucking miracle.

By the time I had finally dragged myself through the doors and out onto the pavement, the rest of our lads had bolted off in different directions and I was left on my own, wondering how the fuck I was going to get home. It was now a quarter to eleven and the train had left a good half an hour ago. Luckily, there was a taxi waiting nearby so I yanked open the door and ordered the driver to take me to Bolton. It was going to cost me an arm and a leg but I didn't care. I wanted to get the fuck away from Blackburn's mob as quickly as I possibly could, irrespective of the cost.

I was aching all over and spattered with blood. The taxi driver must have been wondering what the fuck had happened to me. Still, I bet he was glad of the money and, I'll tell you what, I've never been as glad to pay for a cab as I was that night. Blackburn had done well against us but then again, we had been running amok until the end of the night, which says something about their abilities. They were clearly only capable of getting a result against us when they had the numbers. They are sad bastards for thinking that they are big for picking on eight hooligans. All they proved was that they always wait until we've been split up before they make a move.

Twenty-six of our lads ended up in court due to the events of that day, which meant I was in good company when I turned up at the magistrates for my hearing. The judge gave everybody fines, regardless of what offence they had committed. We probably would have ended up in jail nowadays but you could get away with a lot more back then, thank fuck.

In addition to our fines, we were issued with exclusion orders, banning us from all football grounds in England, Scotland and Wales for a six-month period and forbidding us from attending the European Championships in England later that year. I stayed away from domestic football until the end of the season but there was no chance in hell that I was going to miss the England versus Scotland match at the Euros. They should thank their lucky stars that I obeyed the ban at all, because when you're involved in football violence, you want to be at every single match. It is an addiction like no other, the best buzz in the world, regardless of whether you're fighting the gamest firm in the world or being picked off by Blackburn at the end of the night.

Now that the lads have taken you through three decades of battles with Blackburn, you will surely notice a recurring theme at every game we've played. They only come looking for us when there are more of them than there are of us. Anybody can fare well against a handful of stragglers but it's a different kettle of fish when you're going to war with an army of rival hooligans. Blackburn need to stop picking off little groups of our lads and stand and fight against the lot of us. Until they are willing to fight fair, we will always have a negative opinion of them. They have no-one to blame but themselves.

17
PRESTON

Lancashire may be home to the likes of Blackburn but it is also where the infamous Preston Para Squad is from, which is easily the best firm from round these sides. They are not quite on Bolton's level but they are a small, tight-knit mob that can definitely hold their own. For some strange reason, we always seem to play them either on Boxing Day or in the run up to Christmas, which is handy as it means that we don't have too travel far to get a fight over the festive season. The opportunity to have a brawl with a mob like theirs is the perfect Christmas present as far as I am concerned.

The atmosphere at Bolton versus Preston games is always fiery given the relatively close proximity of the two clubs and the Little Lever lot had a tasty scrap with them in the Nineties, when we had them at home for the last match of the season. Here's Phil to tell you what went down . . .

Phil

This particular game was a little different than usual, as we didn't travel to the match with the rest of Bolton's mob. I set off to the ground with twelve other lads from Little Lever and as we made our way down the road, we noticed a vanload of our opponents stuck in the middle of a traffic jam with nowhere to go. It looked as if we were going to get a fight in fairly early on.

Our rivals were hanging out of the windows of their vehicle, drinking cans of lager and singing Preston songs. There were no Old Bill around and it was the perfect opportunity for a scrap so a lad called Eric walked over to their van to kick it off.

'There's no Old Bill around,' he told them. 'Let's flare it off before the coppers get here.'

One of the passengers in the van started getting mouthy so Eric gave him a crack through the open window, knocking him sprawling onto the driver. A second later, the sliding door at the side of the vehicle came flying open and Preston's lads spilled out onto the street, looking to do some damage. They had left their van in the middle of the road and it was blocking off the traffic behind them but they didn't seem to give a fuck. They were far too busy readying themselves for combat to pay any of the other road users the slightest bit of attention.

As we were going at it with the Preston lot, a group of Bolton lads descended on their van and smashed it to fuck. By the time the Old Bill arrived to put an end to the trouble, their vehicle was in a right state and the traffic had been held up for a good five minutes.

'Quick, scarper,' I yelled to the rest of our lads, not wanting to end up getting nicked before the game had started. We hadn't even got to the ground yet and we had already had a fight. It was shaping up to be a proper exciting day.

We scattered in different directions and met up at the boozer opposite the away end a couple of minutes later. Preston's van came chuntering into the car park shortly after we arrived, looking as if it had been in a high-speed collision. All the windows were smashed and it had big fuck-off dents down the side.

We had a couple of drinks and then we made our way inside the ground. The atmosphere was tense as fuck, with missiles flying about the place and coins clattering against the fence that separated the two sets of supporters. Why do people always throw their money at the opposition? It has always proper baffled me. It's never 1ps and 2ps either, it's always larger denominations.

The game ended up as a 1–0 victory for Bolton and as we made our way back into town to have a celebratory drink, we noticed that the Old Bill had cordoned off Bradshawgate. A couple of coppers were stood about the streets, putting their riot gear on, and there were a few vans parked around the place, indicating that something was definitely going off.

As it turned out, the commotion stemmed from the fact that the Para Squad had decided to go for a drink in our pub. They were chucking glasses, bottles and ashtrays out at our fans and some of our younger lads were running around the streets, bricking our boozer in an attempt to force them out.

The coppers were attempting to direct the regular fans away from the disturbance and into the centre via different roads but, strangely enough, they didn't seem as bothered about our hooligans.

'Go on then,' one of them motioned to us. 'If you want them, go get it.'

And with that, the two police vans moved aside to let us past.

For around two-and-a-half minutes, it was bedlam. Missiles were flying around the place and it was almost as if the coppers were allowing it to happen. Then, as the action reached its peak, they charged in with their horses and their dogs and started beating everybody with their batons. The sneaky bastards had set us up. They had allowed us to kick off and now they were steaming in and nicking as many lads as they could get their hands on.

All in all it was a proper good day, despite the underhand tactics of the Bolton OB. We managed to get some action in both before and after the game and, credit where it's due, Preston had some balls for going into our pub. If the coppers hadn't ruined our fun we would have taught our rivals not to be so cheeky. However, even with the Old Bill there, we had a decent go at the Para Squad and a proper good time was had by all.

I had an equally intense run-in with the Preston boys when we played them at an away game in March 1985. We got the upper hand against them but they gave another impressive performance. I knew that they were going to have a firm out for us, because, even though they rarely travel to ours in numbers, they always have a go at their place.

On the day of the match, I arrived at the station in Bolton to see a mixture of older lads and Bolton Youth lads scattered along the platform. There were quite a few of us there and I was confident that we'd be able to handle whatever our opponents had in store for us. Now all that was needed was for us to get to Preston and find their firm without the coppers putting us in an escort.

There were only a few Old Bill waiting for us at Preston station. That has to go down as an oversight on their part, because we set off to look for our rivals the minute we got off the train. Our first ports of call were the Bull and Royal on Derby Road and the Red Lion on Liverpool Road, as they were Preston's main boozers. We packed out both of their pubs and waited to see if they were going to show their faces.

I spotted a couple of Preston's lads sneaking out of their boozers just after we arrived but rather than going after them, I decided to leave them to it, simply because I knew they would tell the rest of the Para Squad where we were. However, after an hour of waiting, we eventually became impatient and set off towards the ground to see if we could locate them.

We managed to get as far as Preston nick on Ribbleton Lane without getting any trouble off our opponents. Then we caught sight of an eighty-strong mob of Para Squad further down the road. I immediately knew it was on. Preston had a fair few black lads in their firm and they were a mixture of different ages, just like us. We expected them to back away as soon as they got onto us but they didn't seem in the least bit fazed by our presence. They stood their ground and waited.

The Para Squad started off fairly well, despite the fact that we had more boys, although their performance began to suffer after one of their black lads got sparked out. Seeing that a member of their firm was laying on the floor unconscious, they got the jitters and we were able to use their failing morale to our advantage. One of the Bolton boys had a bottle of ammonia on him and he sprayed it into some poor lad's face, causing him to clutch his skin and scream in agony as it burnt into his flesh. The victim was a sorry sight but his cries fell on deaf ears, as the rest of our mob continued to rain a flurry of punches down into him, ignoring his anguished pleas for help.

After a couple of minutes of getting their heads kicked in, Preston decided to make a run for it and we chased them down the street, eager to do them some more damage. However, by this stage, there were a fair few Old Bill on the scene and they soon put a stop to things. Within a relatively short period of time, they managed to shove us into an escort and walked us to the ground to make sure that we couldn't get up to any more high jinks before the match kicked off.

The game itself was less of a result for us as we lost 1–0 but we managed to keep our spirits up by pelting Preston's lads with projectiles.

As soon as the final whistle had gone, a couple of our fans ran out onto the pitch and someone lobbed a smoke bomb down onto the grass. We were pissed off about the result and in the perfect mood for causing chaos.

Sensing that we were going to take our anger out on the Para Squad, the Old Bill kept us in the ground for twenty minutes after the game had finished, hoping it would give us time to calm ourselves down. It was a foolish thing to do, because we turned on them instead, backing them down the steps with the intention of doing them in. Luckily for the coppers, some of their colleagues came steaming over on horseback and we were charged across the terraces before we could get stuck in. There was then a brief standoff between the Cuckoo Boys and the coppers before the gates were finally opened up and we were allowed to leave the stadium.

We left the ground, accompanied by a police escort, and walked straight into the hands of the Para Squad, who were waiting for us on this big park facing Deepdale stadium. Our opponents were giving it the verbals so we ran straight through the Old Bill and laid into them. They immediately backed off and we soon had them on their toes. We legged them all the way across the park and onto Blackpool Road, where we kicked one of the stragglers to fuck. He wasn't the only lad to get hurt, as by this stage the coppers were chasing our lot about the place on horseback and beating them with their truncheons. The plod eventually regained control of the situation after setting dogs on a couple of our lads. We were escorted to the station, where we got the train back home without anything else kicking off.

We had managed to get a result against the Preston lads but they had put up a fair bit of resistance. They could have buggered off while we were being kept behind in the stadium but they chose to front up instead. It was another action-packed day and I doubt the Old Bill will forget it in a hurry. We did exactly what we set out to do. We caused no end of trouble and we gave our opponents a fucking good hiding.

The fact that the Para Squad stood and fought with us on both the occasions described here should give you an indication of what kind of a firm they are. They don't always come out on top but they are always willing to give it a go and that counts for a lot in my book.

They aren't the biggest mob and they aren't the most well-known but they've got a game set of lads with them and they're a handy little crew. They're definitely one of the strongest firms from round our neck of the woods and it was a pleasure to have it with them.

18
'WE'RE ALL OFF TO FIND THE COCKNEYS'

Although our battles with the other northern teams were exciting, the rivalry between the north of England and the south of England could be just as intense. Phil was lucky enough to be part of a united northern firm that got together at England's European Championship game against Scotland on 10 June 1996. Here he is to fill you in on what went down . . .

Phil

On the day of the match, we could hardly contain our excitement. I was travelling down to London with twelve other lads from Little Lever and we were all looking forward to getting stuck into the Jocks. We didn't set out with the intention of teaming up with the other northern firms. It was the last thing on our minds at that point.

We set off at half seven, arrived at half eleven, and parked our van up in one of the capital's many ridiculously overpriced car parks.

'Well,' I thought to myself, 'at least it's going to be safe here and nobody's going to pinch the fucker.'

We decided to travel around the city via the tube, as we had heard it was the best way to get from A to B. However, after heading off in the wrong direction a couple of times without a clue about which train to catch, we began to wonder if we had been given dodgy advice. We eventually ended up in

Trafalgar Square and the minute we left the station we were smack bang in the middle of a thousand-strong crowd of Jocks.

None of us fancied going up against that many rival lads quite yet so we headed off along the road to look for a boozer. A couple of the Sweaty Socks had worked us out and they started bouncing about the streets and throwing bottles at us. Their lads were mingled in with the regular supporters but you could spot them a mile off, because they were as smartly dressed as we were. They were looking as if they were about to flare it off so I braced myself, ready for the spark to ignite.

Just as the situation was about to come to a head, the boys in blue appeared out of nowhere and came steaming over towards us. We backed off into the tube station, where we jumped on a train to Soho in order to get away. Most of the lads headed straight for the strip clubs for a quick gander but my mates and I chose to give it a miss. We sat on the edge of the pavement, sniffing poppers and boozing until the rest of the firm came out. Soho is seedy and shady as fuck. The local coppers walk around the streets in pairs and they all have guns and body armour, which shows what a dodgy place it is. It made us feel proper on edge but going there was definitely an experience.

As soon as the rest of the mob had finished ogling the strippers, we rang the other lads from Bolton that had travelled to London for the game and sorted out a place to meet up. Forty-five lads had made it down, which made me feel a little less uneasy about walking around a strange city.

'Who else is here then?' I asked one of our lads.

'Oxford have got great numbers, as have Forest,' I was told. 'Chelsea have got a lot here but Middlesbrough have got the biggest turnout. They've got a hundred-and-fifty lads with them.'

There were a fair few different mobs about the place, which was good. It meant that there was a greater chance of something kicking off. None of us had tickets so we had a mooch about to try and find a boozer with a decent atmosphere to watch the game in. We eventually settled on a pub that was literally bursting at the seams. It was crowded as fuck but it would have to do.

There was a big group of Sweaty Socks at the opposite side of the pub, which was an immediate source of tension. The atmosphere reached boiling point shortly after England scored. Our rivals looked as if they were going to kick things off so a couple of English lads went over and put in a pre-emptive strike. I wasn't involved myself and none of our lot were caught up in the brawl.

We were left standing there watching the action, which was all well and good until a load of baton-wielding riot police steamed in through the doors and started clearing the English fans out. A couple of lads tried to put up some resistance but they were quickly sorted out. The coppers weren't pissing around. Anybody who disobeyed them got a baton round the head.

As we made our way outside the pub, I noticed a tasty-looking mob on the other side of the road. They must have been at least one-hundred-and-twenty-strong.

'What are they here for, do you reckon?' I asked one of my mates. 'Do you think they were planning on swarming the pub to get at the Jocks before the dibble turned up?'

'Fuck knows,' my mate replied. 'I don't even know who they are.'

After a couple of minutes of scratching our heads, attempting to work out which team the mob belonged to and what they were intending on doing, this big Geordie fella came across to break the ice.

'Where are you lot from?' he asked us, his body language suggesting that we might be in for a spot of bother if we gave the wrong response.

All the lads from the pub were from different towns and cities across the north of England. We filled him in on where we had travelled down from and he lightened up a bit.

'We're all off to find the Cockneys,' the Geordie told us. 'Are you up for joining up with us? Fuck the Jocks. It's Chelsea and the southern firms that we want to do.'

Most of the lads in his mob were from Middlesbrough and they were more interested in a victory for the North over the South than they were in England beating Scotland. It was an exciting prospect. The rivalry between the North and the South is even more fearsome than England versus Scotland. I was well up for it.

After getting some drinks in at a couple of different pubs, the newly formed northern alliance came across some Arsenal lads hanging about at this big park and there was a short bout of violence before the coppers turned up. The Old Bill charged around the place, splitting us all up and pushing us down the street. While we were being shoved about by the coppers, another huge mob gathered at the opposite end of the road.

'Who are you? Who are you?' we chanted, attempting to work out whether they were from the North or the South.

'Chelsea, Chelsea, Chelsea,' they shouted back.

There was no messing about. The minute they heard the response, the Middlesbrough lads went steaming in. The Chelsea lot braced themselves for a row as the entire Northern mob followed Boro's lead. The police presence could do little to stop this epic battle of the regions. It was time for us to settle the North versus South debate once and for all.

Our battle didn't end up being quite as epic as we had anticipated, because more Old Bill turned up on horses thirty seconds after we reached the Cockneys. It was time for us to head off to the bars and lay low until the situation was less on top.

After a couple more pints, we decided to set off back to Bolton. There were too many coppers on the scene for anything else to go off. Word was spreading round that a mob of Forest were looking to do everybody in but we felt that it was too late to go out looking for them. The day was officially over, as far as we were concerned.

Personally, I couldn't give a fuck about the whole North–South thing but I was sick to death of the Southerners trying to claim that their part of the country was better than ours and so the opportunity to represent the North was a real privilege. At the end of the day, everywhere's got plenty of trendy bars and shops but the Londoners seem to think they've got the monopoly on that shit. It was good to get the opportunity to show them what the North was capable of. We might not have anywhere that is as world renowned as Big Ben or Buckingham Palace but we can definitely have a fight. And in the world of football violence, that's the most important thing.

19
BIRMINGHAM CITY ZULUS

Birmingham was another firm that always gave us a tough time. They called themselves the Zulus after the African warrior tribe and they lived up to their nickname 100 per cent. They had a lot of black lads in their ranks and they were, in my opinion, one of the best mobs in the country. They were certainly the best in the Midlands.

Bolton have been done a number of times at Birmingham so when we found out that we were playing Birmingham City at home in February 1990, we were determined to prove to ourselves that we could get one over on them. Things had been pretty quiet, as we had recently endured a set of dawn raids in which thirty-four lads were nicked. Nevertheless, this was a game that no-one could afford to miss. We weren't expecting the Brummies to bring a large following with them but we knew that the lads that they brought would all be game as fuck. We were going to need to be running on full steam in order to stand a chance.

On the day of the match, we met up at the Alma Inn and a couple of the other nearby pubs, ready to show the Zulus what we were made of. We were a bit nervous but we had a fairly decent turnout so we knew we would do all right. Our spotters were positioned around the town centre so that we could get into our opponents as soon as they touched down.

Time went by and we got bored of waiting so a few of us headed over to the Sweet Green Tavern on Crook Street to get some more drinks. We were approaching the boozer when a group of around twenty lads came marching out of the station, chanting, 'Zulu, Zulu'. It was the moment we had been waiting for.

Both mobs went steaming into one another with neither side backing down. One of Birmingham's black lads got twatted in the head with a brick and went down like a sack of potatoes. Another black lad came to his aid but one of our lot slashed him across the face before he had a chance.

As the battle progressed, I began to come unstuck but luckily one of the other Cuckoo Boys stepped in and prevented me from getting too badly beaten. However, by that stage, I was already feeling pretty dazed and my jumper was covered in blood. I glanced around to see how we were doing. Both sides had taken a pounding but Birmingham were backing off a bit. We eventually managed to force them back inside the station but before we had a chance to cement our victory the Old Bill turned up with a load of dogs in tow and chased us all the way down Manny Road. One of the coppers tried to leg me up but I just about managed to get away.

The coppers seemed more concerned with twatting people than they were about defusing the situation. They beat a Bolton lad all over his body and another lad was handcuffed and manhandled onto the floor, despite the fact that he was covered from head to toe in blood. I later found out that he was charged with wounding for slashing one of the Zulus.

Not wanting to be the next one to get nicked, I avoided the town centre for a while and headed off to the Wagon and Horses to get myself cleaned up. I had a quick wash and threw my bloodstained jumper in the bin. I was aching all over but buzzing from the action and hoping that we would get to have another pop at some point during the day. I got a couple of drinks down me and set off for the ground. Part way through the journey, I saw a load of Bolton lads trying to get at a group of a hundred and fifty Zulus. It was looking promising but the coppers had it all wrapped up. They escorted the Brummies across the away car park.

The game itself was fairly uneventful. There were a couple of minor incidents but nothing to write home about. We beat the Brummies 3–1 in the end but the real victory came after the final whistle had blown. As soon as we left the ground, a good three hundred of us plotted up on the side streets near Orlando Bridge and another group of lads went into the Wagon and Horses. The minute the Brummies reached the Manny Road, all hell broke loose. The lads in the pub came out and pelted them with bricks and we went charging down the street to join them. A couple of the Zulus stood and fought but they soon got kicked to fuck. The rest of them went tearing off across the coach park, causing us to turn our attention towards the Old Bill. We were fired up after doing the Brummies and determined to have a row with somebody, whether it was a rival firm or a group of plod.

The action went on for a good twenty minutes until the coppers finally regained control. They arrested over thirty lads for offences including wounding, carrying offensive weapons and serious assault. One of our lot was found in possession of a calling card with the words 'Kick to kill' printed on it.

Birmingham were incensed by our victory, so much so that the following season they put leaflets in all their town-centre pubs inciting their lads to travel to Bolton for revenge. 'The nightmare returns,' the leaflets read, implying they were looking to do to us what we had done to them.

Whereas the Zulus were raging about what had happened, some of the locals were impressed by our performance. The *White Love* fanzine describes it as a 'classic rumble' and notes, 'The Bolton thugs, in greater numbers, were getting the better of it . . . Birmingham fans remembered they had been "run" and for the two seasons following tried to gain their revenge. In fact the following season's encounter at Burnden had to be switched to a Sunday with the entire Greater Manchester Police force out on overtime money.'

Although we managed to do the Brummies on that occasion, they were one of the toughest firms going and they have my total respect. They are formidable opponents and anybody who tries to tell you otherwise is a liar. The fact that they were so intent on vengeance shows you what a mighty reputation they had to uphold. It was an honour to go up against them and beating them will always stick in my mind as one of our greatest accomplishments.

20

IPSWICH

We have to travel right across the country to play them, so you would have thought that Ipswich would pull a decent-sized firm together to make our journey worthwhile. It is a working-class town with some tough estates and their Ipswich Punishment Squad have been described as 'very frightening' by the British Transport Police. This is somewhat confusing, because when we went up against them on 16 March 2000, they couldn't have been less scary if they tried.

On the day of the match, we travelled down by coach and went straight into a pub called the Drum and Monkey at the back of their ground. There were loads of Bolton lads already inside and a few more out the back, which was handy because shortly after we arrived, some rival lads came through from the other room and started ballooning at us. After mouthing off for a while, one of them threw his pint all over one of our lot so we retaliated by pelting him and his mates with glasses and bottles. They ended up covered in beer and broken glass and legged it out of the pub.

We ran out after them but by the time we had got outside, the 'frightening' Ipswich Punishment Squad were nowhere to be seen. To their credit, they showed up half an hour later and put the windows of the pub through but they were back on their toes again the minute we left the boozer. A couple of our shirters were left cut up from the glass.

Ipswich were a right bunch of wankers. They didn't fancy a ruck so they threw their missiles and then fucked off. That was the last we saw of their lads before the game, which was fortunate for them as we would have kicked their heads in for injuring our fans.

We had a couple more beers and then the pub began to empty as everybody started getting off to the game. We made our way to the ground and settled down to watch what was to be the worst-refereed game that I have ever seen in my life. We lost 5–3 in the end, which was all thanks to Barry Knight. He awarded Ipswich three penalties, gave us twelve yellow cards and sent two of our players off. But yet our rivals didn't even get a slap on the wrist for anything they did. In my book Ipswich didn't beat us that day, Barry Knight robbed us.

When the final whistle blew the Ipswich fans invaded the pitch to celebrate. I was surprised they weren't singing 'There's only one Barry Knight', as he was clearly their man of the match. A load of their supporters were bouncing around in front of us and it was a good thing that there was a ton of coppers and stewards there, otherwise we might not have been able to hold ourselves back.

The so-called 'Punishment Squad' didn't want to know. They made no effort to get to us and we couldn't get past the Old Bill to have it with them. They were nowhere to be seen when we got outside either, although some of their shirters got too mouthy for their own good and ended up getting slapped and legged about the place. It was a shit end to the season and the fact that Ipswich had such a crap firm made it even worse, as we didn't get the chance to even up the score. The long haul home was depressing as fuck and the majority of us would have rather stayed at home.

Ipswich was proper disappointing. A substandard referee and a sub-par mob made it a waste of time going there. Punishment Squad my arse; the only punishment that we got was at the hands of Barry Knight.

21
TO HULL AND BACK

Hull is a moody place to go to. It is a big city and there are a lot of rough places there, especially the areas around the docks. Their City Psychos firm are a handy set of lads and they had a big mob with them in the late 1970s and early 1980s, although it seemed to fade away after that. We had a couple of run-ins with the Psychos during the Eighties. It kicked off on the terraces when we played them in the FA Cup in November 1984 and the action spilled onto the pitch. The Old Bill eventually managed to regain order but the incident had already reached the stage where it was seen as worthy of a mention in Andy Nicholls's *Hooligans* book eighteen years later.

'Repeated violence broke out on the terraces and fans clashed on three sides of the ground,' writes Nicholls. 'The fighting spilt onto the pitch, and while the referee continued with the game, the police sent dogs and horses into the Bolton end. This was regarded as a major "result" for the hooligans at Bolton, as Hull were a formidable mob.'

In the late 1980s, we played Hull again and managed to invade their pitch. They didn't even try to stop us. We took the piss that day. It must have been humiliating for them to know that they were powerless to prevent us from running amok in their town.

In November 2008, we were scheduled for an away game against them at the KC Stadium and there was talk of them turning out in force. The memory of what we had done to them was clearly still fresh in their minds. When somebody shows you up like that, it doesn't go away in a hurry. Still, they had managed to work their way up to the top flight for the first time so at least they had something to be happy about.

On the day of the game, we headed to our rivals' city in an assortment of different vehicles. We had three minibuses and a 4x4 and some of us travelled down by train and coach as well. I was in the 4x4 with six of my mates.

When we got to Hull, we parked our car and headed straight for the pub. The city centre was swarming with Old Bill but we just about managed to avoid them. The lads who went by train had arrived in the city before us and they were already in the boozer, sat around drinking their pints. Forty minutes and a fair few beers later, we decided to make our way to the stadium via the back streets in the hope that we would bump into Hull. It was a good twenty-minute walk but we saw neither hide nor hair of them during the entire journey. We were disappointed by their unwillingness to front up, especially as we had been in contact with them over the internet and had prearranged a row.

Although we beat them 1–0, we couldn't help feeling that Hull had robbed us. Their mob was harder to find than Big Foot and we were deprived of the chance to have it with them. To make matters worse, the cheeky bastards tried to claim that it was us that hadn't showed. There is nothing worse than a firm that fails to turn up and then lies about it afterwards. Still, there was always the return match to look forward to in May 2009. Our younger lads had been in touch with Hull's youth firm and the Psychos had told them that they were planning on bringing a mob to the Reebok. I hoped on this occasion they would walk the walk.

Hull's younger lads had said that they were going to bring a coach load of their youth and a coach load of their regular firm.

'Phone us when you get to Huddersfield and we'll give you directions on where to go from there,' one of the Bolton Youth lads instructed them.

Things would have gone according to plan if the Old Bill hadn't got hold of the fella that was supposed to ring us and escorted him all the way to our ground.

'Oh well,' I thought to myself, 'time to hunt them down.'

Rather than heading straight into the middle of Bolton, we stopped off at a boozer on the outskirts of the town, as a couple of the lads were banned from the centre. We were just settling down to drink our pints when word got round that there was a mob of Hull at the Barracuda Bar on Bradshawgate and three of our boys went to have a look. Sure enough, there was a group of Psychos in there, sat around supping their pints. It was looking as if we were going to get to have a row this time round.

'We're Bolton, ring one of these numbers if you want it,' one of our lads briefed them. 'You're going to have to get away from here though because you're all on camera.'

'Do one muppet, jog on,' a mouthy Psycho sneered back.

'Shut the fuck up you prick,' our lad replied, unwilling to take any shit. 'Just phone one of those numbers if you fancy it.'

And with that, the three Boltonians left the pub and headed back to the rest of our firm to tell them what had happened.

Half an hour later, the Hull lads still hadn't rung so a couple of the boys headed over to the Barracuda to see what the deal was. There was no sign of them in the bar so a group of twenty lads went off into the town centre to see if they had gone in any of the other pubs. It didn't take long to find the Psychos. They had got into a fight with some of the locals and they were in a police escort. One of them had started ballooning at a group of regular, non-hooligan drinkers in Durty Gurtys and an angry mob of civilians had chased them out of the pub.

It was the ultimate humiliation. It's one thing needing an escort to protect you from a mob of rival football lads but it's quite another needing one to prevent you from getting your head kicked in by a bunch of random pissheads. It was funny as fuck and although we didn't get the chance to do them ourselves, they still got done by residents of Bolton. The fact that they were turned over by your average, run-of-the-mill Boltonians rather than our firm was a minor detail. The moral of the story is that you shouldn't attempt to kick off on civilians when there's a match on. Maybe next time they'll be a little bit more discerning about who they run their mouths off at.

22
HIBS

Although we very rarely got to play teams from north of the border, our few encounters with Scottish clubs got just as heated as our matches against English sides. Bolton is a strongly patriotic town and most of our supporters tend to favour Rangers over Celtic. We're firmly behind our soldiers whenever there is a conflict so any team whose followers belt out IRA songs isn't likely to have the support of many Boltonians. The Celtic fans tried that shit during a friendly at the Reebok and we did them all over after the match. Bolton is only a twenty-minute drive from Warrington, where the IRA planted a bomb that killed two children in 1993. If you attempt to glorify the perpetrators of an act like that then you deserve to have your head kicked in.

There are a lot of Rangers fans in Bolton. Many of their supporters proclaim their support for the Ulster Defence Association, a loyalist paramilitary organisation opposed to Irish Republican groups. This makes them a popular choice of team round here, as the majority of locals are passionately anti-IRA.

Then there are Hibs, my favourite Scottish team. My uncle used to play for them and they are based in Edinburgh, my place of birth, so I've always had a soft spot for them. When we had it with their Capital City Service firm in July 2009, I decided to sit it out. However another lad, who I shall refer to as 'Mark', was able to fill me in on how we fared. Here's what he's got to say . . .

Mark

When we first heard the news that we were scheduled to play Hibs in a pre-season friendly, we were all proper buzzing. We hardly ever got to play a Scottish team and they had a reputation for having the country's top firm. Hibs are friendly with some lads from Oldham and the word soon got round that somebody from our mob had got the number of a CCS lad off a member of Oldham's Fine Young Casuals firm. Hibs had been planning a meeting for six weeks prior to the match and it looked as if a row was on the cards.

Some of the CCS lads went to Oldham the night before the game and stayed over at the FYC boys' houses. Another coach load travelled down from Edinburgh the following morning. A couple more came by train, another lot came by minibus and a fair few Oldham lads turned out as well.

We headed off into town and word soon got round that a mob of Oldham were plotted up in the Market pub in Stoneclough. A couple of lads rode over on a motorbike to see how many of them there were and they were surprised to see 150–200 CCS in there, because Hibs had told us that they were only bringing fifty lads with them. There were less than fifty of us available that day, as the rest of our mob was scattered about in different pubs in groups of six and seven.

'We could phone whoever isn't here and get them out,' one of our lads suggested.

'They should have all been told to be here in the first place,' somebody else pointed out.

If we had known what types of numbers Hibs and Oldham were going to turn up with we would have rung a lot more people. The situation wasn't looking good.

While we were busy deciding what to do, one of the lads announced that the FYC and the CCS were on their way to the game and scouts were dispatched to Kearsley to see how many of them there were. When our boys arrived, they were confronted by a big fuck-off mob of rival lads, walking towards the station. The Hibs–Oldham alliance would be at the Reebok in no time at all.

'Oi, come here,' one of our scouts bellowed over to the nearest CCS member. 'How many of you are going to the match?'

'All of us.'

'What about those Oldham twats?'

'They're all going too.'

We were going to have our work cut out for us. But luckily we had a plan. We were going to ambush Hibs on the way back to their coach and take them by surprise.

While Hibs and Oldham were busy watching the game, we made our way to the Market, as their coach and their minibus were parked nearby. Somebody slashed the tyres on the minibus and another lad put the coach windows through. They wouldn't be leaving Bolton any time soon.

We intended to wait about in the Market until Hibs arrived but the Old Bill soon got wind that we were there. None of us fancied getting nicked before it kicked off so we left the pub and looked for another place to drink. As we were walking up the street, one of the lads at the front of the mob shouted, 'They're here.' Adrenalin pumped around my body as I legged it down the road to get to where the action was. Three of our lads were already getting stuck into some CCS and FYC. It was on!

Our opponents knocked a couple of our lads down onto the floor but they were quickly dragged back up again by their mates. At the same time we put a fair few Jocks on their arses. Fists and feet were flying about all over the place but we managed to keep our firm relatively tight so that Hibs and Oldham couldn't get in amongst us.

As well as having to defend ourselves against the CCS and the FYC, we had the truncheon-happy Bolton Old Bill to contend with. They were batoning all and sundry in a futile attempt to separate the warring factions. It was all pretty pointless, as there weren't enough of them to make any impact and we just ignored them.

Part way through the brawl, a load more coppers turned up in full riot gear and pushed us back along the street. They were clad in padded jackets and helmets and they were able to confine the CCS and prevent us from getting at them. We stood around chanting 'England, England' at the top of our voices for a while and then we went back into the Market and sat ourselves down in the beer garden.

The Market had stopped serving drinks, which was a pain in the arse. But what was this? A pair of casually dressed lads were walking up the street towards us. Another row was brewing.

'Come on then,' shouted one of the Bolton lot. 'Are we having it or not?'

Bad move. The two 'casuals' were undercover coppers from the Lothian and Borders police force. They pulled out their IDs, as if to say 'you've picked the wrong guys to mess with'.

A couple of minutes later, some genuine Hibs and Oldham lads pulled up in a car and made their way into the Market. One of them went into the toilets, where he was promptly battered by a Bolton lad. The rest of them tried to do a runner. The slowest of their lads got caught and was given such a doing over that he needed surgery on his ankle.

By the time we left the pub, there were a lot of Old Bill about and they had their cameras with them. The Oldham and Hibs boys were escorted to their vehicles and we decided to call it a day and headed off back to Farnworth. As we walked off down the street, we noticed a group of angry CCS banging the wheels of their minibus and hurling abuse at anybody and everybody. Some of our lot were laughing at them and the coppers had to prevent another fight from taking place.

'It's a waste of time changing those tyres,' one of our lads shouted over. 'They're all too drunk to drive. Get them to blow in a bag.'

It was funny as fuck and we were all proper pissing ourselves.

Although they should have brought a foot pump with them, the CCS had definitely provided us with some stiff competition. They brought a big mob with them and they were all fairly game. Saying that though we didn't do too badly, considering that they outnumbered us by at least three to one.

We spoke to the CCS a couple of days later and I warned them about the undercover cops.

'Nah you must be mistaken. They've been coming with us for a while,' one of their lads assured me.

'They definitely are Old Bill,' I told him. 'One of them flashed his ID at us.'

I guess the coppers must have done a pretty good job. The Jocks seemed convinced that their Lothian police-force pals were genuine hooligans. Once I'd finished persuading the CCS that they had been taken in, the conversation turned to the fight near to where their coach was parked.

'You did well against us,' they said. 'You had a lot of game lads with you. You should come up here and see a game sometime.'

The respect was mutual. Hibs have got a handy set of lads. They turned out a fucking army and provided us with a battle and a half. They're definitely one of the top firms in Scotland and we're looking forward to the next time our two mobs meet.

'A group of forty Hibs fans were returning to their minibus when fighting broke out,' wrote Chris Marshall in the *Edinburgh Evening News*. 'Eyewitnesses said the Hibs fans' minibus was vandalised to stop them escaping.'

'All these taxis turning up didn't make any sense,' a resident of Kearsley told a reporter for the *Bolton Evening News*. 'It's a quiet village down here, and stuff like this doesn't normally happen.'

Well at least we brought a little bit of excitement into the lives of the locals. It will no doubt be the talk of the town for years to come. The people of Kearsley won't forget the Capital City Service in a while. And neither will we because they brought a decent set of lads with them.

23
STOKE

Stoke's Naughty Forty firm were another formidable opponent. BBC News has described them as 'one of the most active and organised football hooligan firms in England'. And not without good reason. Here's Phil to tell you about his run-in with them during the Nineties . . .

Phil

Stoke's old stadium, the Victoria Ground, was always a dodgy place to go to, as it was very close to the motorway. The location had obvious advantages, as it made it easy to get to, but it also had its pitfalls. Just as you thought you had got away without getting hurt, you would look ahead of you on the road and there would be groups of lads hurling bricks and concrete slabs off the bridges. That was their little leaving present. It was a way of saying, 'Thanks for visiting Stoke. Now fuck off and don't come back.'

Things could get just as naughty when Stoke came to Burnden Park. One game in particular was complete and utter bedlam. It was a Saturday match and we knew what time the trains came in from Stoke so, every time that one was due in, a group of lads would wander over to the station to see if the Naughty Forty were on it.

Sure enough, at half-past two, one of our spotters came running into the pub to tell us that our opponents had touched down. We positioned two hundred-odd lads at the top of the road and waited for them to come out of the station. A couple of minutes later, a three hundred-strong mob came pouring out of the entrance. The moment they realised that we were there, it was on. They came pounding down the road towards us and an epic brawl ensued.

It's hard to even describe just how crazy things got. The road was filled with traffic and lads were repeatedly thrown over car bonnets and slammed into the side of parked cars. The coppers eventually regained control of the streets but, by that stage, we'd had our fun. The image of five hundred lads scrapping away will stick with me until my dying day.

Things were a hell of a lot quieter after the match, because in order to prevent a repeat of what had happened earlier in the day the Old Bill drafted in reinforcements from all over the north-west. They even had police helicopters circling around, which only added to our excitement.

There were so many Old Bill swarming around the town that it would have been impossible for another major disturbance to take place. Bolton games were usually very heavily policed, which meant we had to think of ways to avoid it being too on top. The streets were awash with blue and white that day. There were far too many of them there for anything else to go off so we decided to head for home.

I was present for a similarly intense battle with the lads from Stoke in October 1990. It was a home game and a mob of Bolton had gathered in Trotters and the Alma Inn, waiting for our rivals to touch down. I was sitting drinking my pint when all of a sudden the boozer started emptying. Stoke had arrived. It was time to see what they were made of.

A good hundred Naughty Forty lads had touched down and as the two firms went steaming into one another, a volley of glasses and bottles flew through the air. The sound of breaking glass resounded around the streets and we momentarily backed away before coming straight back at them with chairs, bottles and glasses. The fighting quickly spilled over into the road and lads were running about in between the cars, twatting one another. We were fairly evenly matched but Stoke eventually managed to back us off into the pub and put the windows through to try and get at us. We retaliated by chucking tables and chairs back out at our rivals and tooled ourselves up with glasses and bottles, ready to have another pop at them. As we piled out of the pub, armed to the teeth and ready to even the score, our opponents backed off.

We ran them along the road to the corner of Trinity Street, where they managed to get their act together and stood their ground against us.

At this point a proper toe-to-toe brawl ensued, with neither firm willing to back down. Lads from both mobs hit the deck and some of them lay there on the floor unconscious as the battle raged around them. There were no Old Bill in sight and the action seemed to be going on and on.

After what seemed like an eternity, the coppers eventually showed up to put a stop to things. They pushed us back up Bradshawgate and herded Stoke down Manny Road, towards the ground. The bodies of the lads that had been knocked out were still littering the floor and there was a rumour that one of the Stoke boys was dead. Thank fuck it was just a rumour, as the last thing any of us would have wanted was for anybody to lose his life.

There has been a lot of conjecture about what went on that day. In Stoke's book, *Naughty: the Story of a Football Hooligan Gang*, one of their lads claims that they got the upper hand. A lot of our lads disagree and say that we came out on top but personally I think each side gets a point for a draw. 100 per cent respect to everybody involved, because it was a fearsome battle and Stoke have definitely got a decent set of lads with them.

24
DONCASTER

Doncaster isn't exactly top of the list when it comes to places associated with football violence. They lack the hooligan credentials of some of the larger teams but they can definitely have a row and we've had a fair few good run-ins with them. Their firm are called the Doncaster Defence Regiment, because they are quite a small firm and often find themselves having to protect their town against a mob with a lot more lads at its disposal. One of our fiercest battles with them took place in the 1980s at an away game. Here's S to fill you in on what went down . . .

S

On the day of the match, ten Little Lever lads met up in Coronation Square. We didn't expect much from Doncaster, mainly because we didn't even know that they had a mob. As we boarded the bus into Bolton town centre, most of the lads were chattering excitedly to one another about what a good piss up we were going to have. We were completely oblivious to the fact that our opposition were going to stand and fight.

When we got to the station, some of us paid for tickets but the majority jumped the barriers. There were a good hundred-and-fifty lads waiting for us on the platform, an impressive turnout considering that we didn't think that we were going to get any trouble. The train pulled in and everybody rushed to get a seat. We had to change at Manchester Piccadilly and there were a fair few Old Bill there but they left us well alone. The connecting train for the second leg of our journey arrived and we all got on.

DONCASTER

When we finally reached the station at Doncaster, we were met by more Old Bill. They searched us for weapons and then allowed us into the town centre, which was a major error of judgement, as we would go on to cause untold devastation. We found a pub near a roundabout, not too far from the ground, and we were just settling down to get a couple of beers in before the match when a carload of our lads turned up.

'We've just spotted a boozer with a mob of Doncaster lads drinking outside,' one of them told me. 'Drink up and we'll go and kick it off with them.'

We downed our pints in unison and marched off like soldiers across the roundabout, heading towards the boozer where our enemies were plotted up. As we approached the pub, glasses started raining down on us so we mobbed up and charged in the direction they were coming from. The DDR seemed to know that we were coming and I suspect that someone might have tipped them off.

A raging battle ensued and the contents of a pool table were emptied and used as weapons. We fought toe to toe with our opponents for what seemed like forever. The Doncaster lads were game as fuck and showed no sign of backing down. The Old Bill eventually turned up to put a stop to things but, by that stage, the damage was done. The streets were strewn with broken glass, pool balls and pools of blood. Some of our lads were badly cut up and their clothes were ripped. But that's all part of the fun.

There were twelve arrests altogether and four of our lot were kept on remand in Armley prison in Leeds, which is now known as HMP Leeds. They were charged with violent disorder and affray. There were skirmishes throughout the day but that was the fiercest battle. Respect to the Doncaster lads for transforming what we had originally thought was going to be a trouble-free day into a row and a half.

S's story just goes to show that you should never underestimate an opponent. It's not the only time we've had a run-in with the Donny lot. When we played them in the FA Cup in January 2007 they put up a fair bit of resistance. It was another game in which the Old Bill took a couple of our lads in but it was worth it, considering the fun we had.

On the day of the match, four hundred of us gathered at Bolton train station. All of the old faces were there and there were a lot of youngish lads thrown into the mix. Everybody was in a good mood and the booze was flowing in typical Bolton fashion. We carried on drinking all throughout the journey and when we arrived in Donny the Old Bill were considerate enough to have a welcome committee there to greet us. The platform was packed with coppers and they had their dogs with them, ready to set them on us at the slightest hint of trouble. It was a bit over the top if you ask me.

Some of the lads got out of the station without the OB getting a grip of them but the majority of them were herded towards one end of the platform.

'In the bubble,' shouted one of the coppers. 'Put them in the bubble.'

The 'bubble' was the Old Bill's word for a large circle of plod. Once they had successfully surrounded us, they kept us in place for what seemed like forever while their colleagues cleared a path for us across the platform. They then formed two lines of officers, leading all the way to a set of buses outside the station. We were herded along the middle of these two lines to make sure that nobody could slip away. Once we were on the buses, we were driven to a large pub not far from the ground. It was rammed to capacity but the Old Bill kept shoving more and more lads inside until it was bursting at the seams. Coppers were stationed at every available exit, some on horseback and some with dogs.

When it was finally time to set off to the ground, the OB ordered everybody out of the pub and escorted us all the way there. However, despite the coppers' efforts to prevent us from enjoying ourselves, some of the Bolton lot still managed to fuck the game off and went into a pub near the ground, where they were able to have a scrap with a couple of Donny lads. Word got round to a few of the lads who were inside the ground but by the time they arrived on the scene, the Donny boys had already fucked off.

The game itself was boring as fuck so twenty of us got off at half-time. We left the stadium just in time to see the lads who had been in the pub travelling into the town centre on a bus. Wanting to catch up with them we hopped on the next available bus but when we finally managed to find them, they had already got into another scrape with the Regiment. The Old Bill had arrived on the scene yet again and the action had been brought to a halt. We had only just been filled in on what happened when the street suddenly filled up with police cars and a double-decker bus pulled up at the side of the road.

'Get on the bus,' a copper instructed us. 'It'll take you back to the station. We don't want any more trouble from you lot.'

We did as he instructed and we were greeted by yet another line of Old Bill, waiting for us at the station. They were being their usual wankery selves, doing their utmost to wind us up. A few of our lads ended up getting nicked for fuck all. The rest of us were shoved onto a train heading back to Bolton via Manchester.

The plod were leaving nothing to chance. They didn't want anything to go off on the train so they filled our carriage with Old Bill. It was a shame because there were loads of Swansea lads on the platform when the train stopped at Sheffield but, try as we might, we couldn't get past the coppers to get to them. Those cunts were wading into everybody with their batons and there was no chance of giving them the slip.

Some of the lads managed to get off the train at Manchester and do one up the platform but the majority had to stay where they were. We were confined to our carriage all the way to Bolton, which put an end to the day's festivities. And to add insult to injury, ten of our lads got a knock on their front doors from the Old Bill further down the line. The coppers tried to claim that the incident at the pub had been organised beforehand, which was obviously a load of bollocks, so, thankfully, the charges were eventually dropped.

All in all, it was a good day out but it could have been a lot better if it wasn't for the Old Bill. We had missed out on rows with both Doncaster and Swansea, which was disappointing given that the other Bolton lads did manage to have it with the Donny lot. Doncaster may not have the world's best-known firm but they were proper up for it and they've got some game lads. Credit where it's due, they were a lot better than we expected so respect to them for that.

25

OLDHAM

Donny surprised us by turning out because we didn't even know they had a mob, Oldham surprised us because we thought they were shit but ended up being all right. We had always viewed them as a tinpot firm up until our away game against them in January 1983. In the 1970s we had repeatedly taken their end so we weren't expecting much from them.

On the day of the match, fifty of us got a bus into Oldham, as we figured that the coppers would be expecting us to go by train. The Old Bill were swarming all over the town centre so we headed for a boozer called the Spotted Cow, which is on the outskirts of town. After a couple of pints, we decided that we were going to have to go in Oldham's end in order to get a row. There was zero chance of bumping into their lads in the centre, as I have never in all my years of going to the football seen a mob of Oldham out in town.

We were walking through an estate when we saw a mob of seventy to eighty lads heading down the street towards us. At first we assumed they were Bolton because we weren't expecting Oldham to have that many with them.

'Oldham,' they bellowed, and with that, they came storming into us, backing us off down the road. They stopped halfway down the street, giving us just enough time to recover from the shock. Had we been run by Oldham? We couldn't get our heads round it. We were shocked and pissed off. We couldn't have a shitty little firm like theirs chasing us about the place so some of our lads ripped a load of garden fences up, ready to set about them. Other members of our firm picked up stones from a nearby rockery and one lad armed himself with a crate of milk bottles.

Now that we were tooled up, the odds were a little more even. We were outnumbered but that wasn't going to prevent us from defending our pride. In a split second, the battle had resumed and we were fighting toe to toe. Oldham had a black lad with them who looked to be their top boy. He was at the forefront of everything they did and was game as fuck but he ended up getting sparked out over the rockery and their morale began to evaporate. We backed them up the road and some of them darted off through people's gardens in an attempt to get away. Victory was in sight.

Our opponents were soon either lying on the floor covered in blood or making a hasty retreat. We legged them nearly all the way to the ground and some of our lads went in their end. A couple of our lot got nicked and a couple of others were escorted back round the pitch into the Bolton section. We had done our rivals before the game and during the game, now all that was left was for us to do them in again once the match had finished.

After the game, we ran round to the home end and legged the Oldham lot up the side streets. They had had their fill for the day and they didn't want another beating, although I have got to take my hat off to them because they were proper on point that day. They would have done us easily if we hadn't been tooled up. It was weird because they usually don't want to know unless they've got another firm with them. They're a bit of a rent-a-mob. In the 1970s they tagged along with a couple of Man U, in the late 1980s and early 1990s they joined forces with Hibs and nowadays I've heard that they take lads from Shrewsbury and Stockport with them.

It would be easy to say that Oldham's performance that day has changed my opinion of them but it was an anomaly. Their general standard is poor. The only other time they put up any resistance when I've been there was during a game against Gillingham, when a handful of them went in the Burnden paddock, shouted 'Oldham' and then hid behind the Old Bill. Mind you, Phil informs me that they turned out a mob for us in the Nineties during an FA Cup match at our place. Here's his account of what went down that day . . .

Phil

It looked as if it was going to be a fairly uneventful day at first, as there was no sign of trouble before or during the game. Then Oldham scored a goal and the atmosphere took a turn for the worse. Those cunts had knocked us out of the FA Cup and we were determined to take our revenge as soon as the final whistle had blown.

After the match had finished, both sets of supporters were let out of the stadium at the same time, although the coppers kept fifty of our lads penned together to prevent them from causing trouble. Then, as we made our way back towards Bolton town centre, a line of riot vans, dog handlers and horses assembled to keep the rival groups of fans on opposite sides of the road. The streets were dark and rainy and the sound of police dogs barking and sirens screeching echoed through the air. It could go off at any time.

Part way through our journey away from the ground, the police stopped to decide what they were going to do next. A couple of Oldham lads and a couple of Bolton lads started bouncing around in the middle of the road, taking advantage of the pause in the proceedings. They looked as if they were contemplating whether to get into one another or whether to wait for a better time to strike.

A few quick punches were exchanged but the Old Bill soon got the situation under control again. It was a busy Saturday and the streets were filled with shoppers. The passers-by must have been wondering what the fuck was going on.

The coppers carried on escorting us until we reached a posh hotel called the Pack Horse, which is on Nelson Square. Then, all of a sudden, all hell broke loose. Both sets of fans went charging into one another and the OB started throwing people into vans in a desperate attempt to prevent us from going at it. That only made things worse, because we ended up having running battles with the police as well as with our rivals.

The violence eventually subsided and the two mobs went their separate ways. It had gone off big style but it could have been a damn sight worse, as the following Monday the Bolton Evening News *ran a story stating that sixty Oldham lads had been stopped en route to Bolton at ten o'clock in the morning, armed with a frightening array of tools. CS gas, ammonia, knives and bats were uncovered and the Football Intelligence Unit hailed the seizure as a major success.*

Even the hardest and most respected members of our firm had to admit that they were glad the tooled-up Oldham lads had been caught. They could have inflicted serious injuries and, who knows, it might even have been me. As it was, we got to have a fight and nothing too horrific went down. All things considered, it was a good day out.

It sounds like Oldham were up for it that day but that certainly isn't the norm. They are far from the strongest firm we've come up against, although every dog has its day. Fair play to the handful of lads who actually want a fight. Every mob has its heroes and its cowards and I guess that Oldham just has a lot more of the latter.

26

MILLWALL

So far I've written about our most fearsome rivalries, our biggest grudge matches and our fiercest battles but no football-hooligan book would be complete without a chapter on the most iconic mob of them all. Millwall's world-famous Bushwhackers. They call Millwall's ground The Den for a reason. They're a bunch of fucking animals and they'll defend their patch to the death. Our Great Lever lad went up against them at home and is lucky enough to have survived to tell the tale . . .

GLL

No matter what anybody says about Millwall, they were definitely one of the top firms in the country and I was really looking forward to the match. It was January 1975 and Bolton had got their act together by this stage, spurred on by our kicking at the hands of Man U the previous year. We had improved our organisation and we were running on full steam, although the prospect of going up against the Bushwhackers was still daunting. My stomach was full of butterflies and I was as much afraid as I was excited.

On the day of the match, I arrived in town at midday and there were already large numbers of our boys hanging around on Bradshawgate. I made my way over to the Prince Bill pub and there were even more lads in there. It is always good to have a sizeable mob behind you when you are up against a team like Millwall and it helped to put my mind at rest. At half two, word got round that Millwall's train had pulled in at the station and my knees started knocking. My spine was tingling and my stomach felt funny. It was time for us to find out if the stories were true.

The Old Bill blocked off parts of Bradshawgate with horses and dogs while our rivals were escorted down the Manny Road. There were a good three hundred of them and they were all in their thirties and forties.

'What the fucking hell is that?' we chanted, trying to make out that they were nothing to us. Inside however it was a different story. We knew that we would have our work cut out when it went off.

'Did you come in a taxi?'

If they did then it must have been a fucking big one.

The Bushwhackers were raring to get at us and they attempted to run through the Old Bill to have it, although it was only ever a token gesture given the number of coppers on hand. We responded by chucking a couple of missiles at them, which was our only option at that point. It looked as if we were going to have to bide our time until the Old Bill fucked off.

Once we had got inside the ground, we were finally able to get at them, as a small group of Bushwhackers had bravely decided to come into our end. There were only ten of them but they were game and they didn't seem to be fazed by our superior numbers. Saying that though, most of them ended up getting kicked to fuck and the rest of them got chased out onto the pitch. One of their lads had to be carried out of the stand on a stretcher and he'll probably think twice before he tries to come into our end again.

There were disturbances all throughout the game, mainly in the Embankment End where both sets of fans were kicking the living daylights out of one another for the full ninety minutes. Being brutally honest, Millwall eventually got the better of us and it was only the intervention of the coppers that stopped us from getting battered. The Bushwhackers were shaping up to be one of the strongest mobs we had taken on, although their morals left a lot to be desired. A rumour went round that one of their lads slashed a girl in the face during the commotion, which is a proper cowardly thing to do. You can't go around cutting innocent women up and expect to get away with it.

By the time the final whistle had blown, we were dying to get outside so that we could punish the Bushwhackers for taking such a liberty. There were so many of us waiting for them after the game had finished that we completely filled one side of the road. The coppers were being their usual *heavy-handed selves by charging us with their horses so we retaliated by pelting them with projectiles. One of the OB got hit on the head with a brick, much to the delight of our firm. If you go around ploughing an animal that weighs half a ton into people you can hardly expect them to take it.*

For some unknown reason, the authorities decided to open up the gate and let the Millwall supporters out while we were in the middle of the road chucking missiles up at the cops. There was a rallying cry of 'Millwall, Millwall' and the next thing I knew, the Bushwhackers were on us, punching and kicking for all they were worth.

Those Cockney twats got fucking leathered. One of them got butted in the face and he dropped like a stone. A couple more ended up on the floor, getting kicked all over. There were far too many of us there for them to stand a chance and after a good few minutes of us battering them, they were sprinting up the road to the station. The most notorious firm in the country had crumbled.

Seeing the famous Bushwhackers getting such a kicking gave me a funny feeling at the base of my spine. We were doing Millwall . . . and it felt good. Some of them were begging the Old Bill for protection and the rest of them were desperately trying to get away. We had broken them mentally and now all that was left was for us to break them physically.

The coppers eventually managed to get the situation under control but, by that stage, the mighty Bushwhackers had been leathered to fuck. As the plod escorted them to the station, we bombarded them with missiles, revelling in our victory. We had emerged triumphant after going up against one of the best firms in the country. Not only had we beaten them but we had also given them one of the worst hidings I have ever seen.

The Bolton boys earned their stripes that day but that's not taking anything away from Millwall, as they have given it to us over and over again at the Den throughout the years. They are one game set of lads but every firm gets beaten every now and then and I doubt if they will ever forget the pasting they got at Bolton. It was a game I will remember for the rest of my life. It is not every day that you get to beat a legendary mob. If you are willing to give it your all then victory can be yours, no matter who you are up against.

Millwall's firm are probably better known than their team but that has never dissuaded them from fighting for their club. Whether they are home or away, we are always guaranteed a scrap and they have forged a reputation that nobody can take away. Few mobs strike fear into the hearts of hardened football lads like the Bushwhackers. They've got a top-class firm and I have got the utmost respect for them.

Whereas it was perfectly understandable for our Great Lever lad to feel uneasy about going up against Millwall, there have been times when we've come up against a lesser-known mob that has managed to run us. It doesn't always take a super-firm to make us lose our resolve. Sometimes all it takes is a mob with superior numbers, along with the advantage of taking us on in their own backyard.

27

THE JACKS

Much as I would like to say that we are the firm that has never run away, that wouldn't be entirely truthful. Sometimes our setbacks have come against superior opponents, whereas on other occasions we have gone to pieces when we really shouldn't have done. However, for every time that we have been run by a firm that we should have stood and fought, there has been an incident when we would have had to be crazy to stick around. It is always embarrassing to run away but sometimes there is no other option available and there is a big difference between losing your bottle and knowing when to make a hasty retreat. When Swansea's Jack Army forced us to do a runner back in 1990, there was nothing else we could have done. Phil was there at a time and he maintains that we had no choice but to make a speedy exit . . .

Phil

When I first heard that we were up against the Jacks at their place, I was apprehensive. I was only seventeen and I had heard that Swansea could be a proper moody place to play at, what with the whole England–Wales rivalry. I was easily intimidated at that age and I was worried that we were going to come unstuck.

To make matters worse, some clever bastard had decided to hire a transit van with 'Little Lever Van Hire' plastered across the side, advertising the fact that we were from Bolton to anybody who wanted to have a pop. Travelling down in that thing would be like walking through the middle of Liverpool, carrying a placard that read, 'I hate Scousers'.

We managed to get to the ground in one piece and we jumped out of the van, leaving a lad called Tony to look for somewhere to park. There had been no disturbances in the run-up to the game and there was only a brief window for the Jacks to get at us while we were making our way out of the stadium.

We won 2–1 and there were a couple of minor disturbances as we were leaving the ground but nothing to write home about. Swansea's firm had left our van completely untouched, despite the fact that Tony parked it proper near to their end. It had been left next to a set of road works so there was plenty of material available if they had wanted to wreck it. It was a miracle it was still in one piece.

Just as we were beginning to think it was our lucky day, Tony attempted to start the van up and was shocked to find that it wouldn't budge an inch. By this stage, a fifty-strong group of Jacks had realised who we were and were making their way across the car park towards us. We might have avoided getting our van smashed up but it was looking as if we were about to get our heads kicked in. There were only fifteen of us and we didn't fancy our chances.

A couple of us started advancing towards the Jacks only for a police van to turn up completely out of the blue. A lone copper jumped out in front of us, brandishing a canine and warning us to stay back. If he had been on his own we would have ignored him but none of us wanted to get on the wrong side of the dog so we did as we were told. The copper managed to hold our rivals off until we found out what was wrong with our van. The H.T. lead had disconnected itself, which was a fairly easy thing to fix and we soon got the engine running.

'Get back in your vehicle,' the copper ordered, in a frantic tone.

We decided it was best to do as he said, not least because the presence of the police dog was the only thing preventing us from getting done in. A lad called Liam was one of the last members of our firm to clamber inside the van. As he was getting in the back, he rammed a lump of breezeblock into the face of one of the Jacks. Swansea, as you can imagine, were enraged and they pelted us with whatever they could get their hands on. Liam retaliated by swinging a plug socket out of the back door and whipping them with it, which goes to show that you can turn practically anything into a weapon if you are inventive enough.

The copper must have radioed for back up, because a few more police vans turned up a couple of seconds later. The Old Bill were now in a better position to put a stop to things and they did their best to get us on our way back home before the situation got any worse.

'You lot follow me in my van and I'll keep you out of trouble,' one of the coppers barked.

We didn't want to end up shadowing the dibble but, then again, we didn't have a whole lot of choice so we grudgingly did as he commanded. We started off by compliantly following the copper as he escorted us through Swansea, but, part way through the journey, Tony became restless and decided that he'd had enough.

'This guy can fuck right off,' he said, swerving the car off in a completely random direction. 'I'm not driving around behind that cunt all day.'

As it turned out, we should have carried on following the Old Bill, because the next thing we knew we were stuck in the middle of a traffic jam on the dual carriageway and there were forty to fifty Swansea lads loitering around on the pavement at the side of us.

'I don't like this,' I said to Tony.

They were arming themselves with projectiles, ready to pelt our van. We had got ourselves into a real predicament. The situation was getting more and more intimidating and our rivals began advancing towards our vehicle, banging on the windows like a set of angry baboons at a safari park. They knew full well that they could take our van whenever the mood took them. They were toying with us before finally going in for the kill.

'Right, fuck this,' Tony exclaimed, driving us up onto a grassy verge and swerving the vehicle across the divide that separated us from the other carriageway. We ended up on the wrong side of the road but after a couple of minutes of dodging oncoming traffic, we managed to turn the van around. We were able to speed off out of Swansea, mopping the sweat from our brows as we went.

It was a narrow escape and we were relieved to have made it out of there in one piece. If Tony hadn't taken action then God knows what our rivals would have done to us. Some of those Taffies are fucking crazy and they really don't like the English. They would have torn us limb from limb.

If we had been on foot then we might have stood a chance against the Jacks but because we were in a van it meant we couldn't effectively defend ourselves. Sometimes you have got no choice but to do a runner and there is no shame in getting off when you would probably end up in hospital by *staying put. We had been brave enough to park a van at Swansea's end with 'Little Lever Van Hire' emblazoned on it so you can't question our bottle. Even though we ended up on our toes, it was an exciting day out and it gave us some great stories to tell our mates back home.*

So there you have it, we have run away when we should have stood and fought and we have run away when we had good reason to run. Every other firm in the country has had similar experiences, although only a handful would ever talk about them as candidly as us.

28

WIGAN

Whereas every firm has done a runner at some point, there is a major difference between losing your bottle during a confrontation and failing to show your face in the first place. Certain firms pretend to be on our level but are secretly scared to face us. Blackburn are the obvious example, as I've already said. You can't get a fight with them in Blackburn, never mind in Bolton. And then there's that pathetic bunch of wankers the Wigan Goon Squad. They are always quick to kick off on our shirters but yet they are unwilling to bring a mob to Bolton.

A 'goon' is a slang term for a dickhead so the name 'Goon Squad' sums up Wigan's firm to a tee. They are renowned for using knives and they are a bunch of fucking bullies. They are all too happy to pick off little groups but when it comes to mob-on-mob action, they don't want to know.

The majority of the battles we've had with Wigan have been at their place, as they are reluctant to come to us. Yet we have still ended up beating the fuck out of them whenever they cross our path. The only time they ever managed to do anything against us was in March 1986, when they slashed up one of our lads at an away game. It was typical of Wigan; they can't fight with their fists.

On the morning of the incident, two hundred and fifty of Bolton's main faces had met up at the station, ready to get the train to Wigan. As far as we were concerned, it was just another away game, although the Goon Squad have always fucking hated us for some unknown reason so they probably saw it as a major grudge match. We have had a lot of lads from Wigan in our firm over the years and I genuinely haven't got anything against the place, other than the fact that it's got a shit set of hooligans attached to it. It's hard to put my finger on the reason for their animosity towards us but whatever the cause, it didn't exactly spur them on to hunt us down. They were nowhere to be seen when our train pulled into the station.

The minute we arrived in Wigan, we sent our spotters off to find their firm. There was a rumour going around that they had a hundred-odd lads with them and we were raring to get at them. If they wanted to have a grudge match then that was exactly what they were going to get. We began to grow impatient and headed off into Wigan town centre. We went bowling through their town as a single massive mob and I can remember feeling an immense sense of pride, as if we were the British army, marching into enemy territory. Now it was just a matter of locating them.

The Goon Squad were nowhere to be seen, which was typical fucking Wigan. It felt like a giant game of hide and seek. Rather than hanging around and waiting for them to arrive, we decided to split up into groups of thirty and head off to different pubs. We knew they preferred to pick off smaller groups. It was the only sure way to get them to front up.

Sure enough, we had been drinking in a pub called the Market Tavern for all of twenty minutes when there was a loud smashing noise and all of the windows went through. It was funny how they managed to find us so quickly when there were only a handful of us. We retaliated by throwing chairs and bottles and a couple of our boys went rushing round to the door to get at them.

As usual the Goon Squad had come tooled up and a Bolton lad called Big G got his back sliced open while he was trying to get out through the doorway to have it with them. He lost a lot of blood and needed over a hundred stitches to fasten up his wound. As if the fact that one of our mates had been slashed up wasn't bad enough, a load of coppers arrived on the scene and started indiscriminately batoning us as we attempted to get out of the pub. A couple of our lads ended up covered in blood and the boozer got trashed from top to bottom.

Big G was eventually hoisted into the back of an ambulance and rushed off to the nearest hospital to have his injuries looked at. He had been cut to fuck and was in a really bad way. By this stage, Wigan were nowhere to be seen, which was lucky for them, as we would have torn them limb from limb. We were proper angry about what they'd done to our mate and wanted to do the same to them.

Much as I disapproved of them using a blade, I had to give Wigan credit for their raid on our pub. Knife or no knife, they successfully ambushed us when we were separated from the main body of our firm. It was the first and only time they did anything of note against us and it made us even more determined to batter them.

By the time we had made our way to the ground, the news that the Goon Squad had slashed Big G up had spread around our firm and a couple of hundred Bolton lads slapped their mob around their end. Wigan kept a very low profile throughout the game. They knew that they had overstepped the mark and they were afraid of what we were going to do. We won the game 3–1 and we took over their ground. We got a result both on and off the pitch and we didn't have to use a knife to do it.

We hung about in Wigan for a couple of hours after the game had finished but the Goon Squad lads were nowhere to be seen. The Old Bill herded us all together and put us on our train. Our revenge against their firm would have to wait until we played them in the Freight Rover area final a couple of months down the line. They couldn't hide from us forever and the fact that we were unable to get even with them immediately after the slashing added fuel to the flames. We were about to teach those cunts a lesson they were never going to forget.

There were two legs of the Freight Rover final. The first leg was at Wigan on 6 May and the second was at Bolton three days later. We knew that Wigan wouldn't come to our place in numbers so our only hope of avenging our fallen comrade was to turn them over at the away game. We would normally go fairly easy on the Goon Squad as they never had a particularly good turnout but this time round there would be no holding back. We were going to kick them to fuck, irrespective of whether they had three lads or thirty thousand lads out.

The game was on a Tuesday night and every nutter in Bolton turned out, looking for a piece of the action. We had it all planned out.

We were going to leave the train at Ince to avoid the Old Bill getting onto us and walk to Wigan's main boozer, the Ball and Boot. They had taken our pub so it was only right that we returned the favour.

A couple of coppers started following us as soon as we got out of the station so we broke out into a run and managed to shake them off. We carried on legging it along the street until we were in spitting distance of our rivals' boozer and then we slowed down to a walking pace. We could see a couple of their lads stood outside their pub, drinking their pints in the distance. We were buzzing about doing them.

The minute they saw us coming, all the Wigan lads bolted inside their boozer and tried to lock us out. We put the windows in and threw a couple of rocks through into the pub and their entire mob shat itself. Some of them scurried underneath the tables and the rest of them positioned themselves against the doors so that we couldn't barge our way in. They were petrified.

A handful of Old Bill had managed to follow us to the pub and they were just as scared as Wigan. They were frantically lashing out with their batons in a desperate attempt to regain control. Just as I was beginning to think that the situation couldn't get any more hectic, there was a sudden roaring noise behind me. I turned round and saw a small firm of Goon Squad lads come tearing through a nearby housing estate. It was the coppers' worst nightmare. They were caught up in the middle of a full-scale riot and were powerless stop to it.

Hundreds of Bolton lads charged at Wigan's supposed reinforcements and the new arrivals did a three hundred and sixty-degree turn and ran for their lives. A couple of them got caught and ended up getting kicked to fuck on the floor. They hadn't shown Big G any mercy so we weren't going to display any towards them. They were a bunch of dirty, cowardly bastards and deserved as good as they got and then some. A load more Old Bill turned up with some canine units in tow and we decided that it was time to make a move. We headed off to the ground, smashing things up and overturning cars as we went.

There were already a good few hundred Bolton lads in the Wigan end by the time we got inside the stadium and we effortlessly slapped the Goon Squad around for the full ninety minutes, despite the fact that they were completely surrounded by coppers. Wigan only had sixty lads with them and some of them ran out onto the pitch to save themselves from getting done. They had been brave enough when they were cutting Big G's back up as he struggled to get outside the pub but now that it was mob versus mob their bottle had mysteriously gone missing. We beat them 1–0 and, as the final whistle sounded, we ran them all the way out of the ground.

The majority of Wigan's firm managed to get away but one of their stragglers tripped and fell. He was quickly beaten unconscious. We waited around in the centre for the rest of the Goon Squad to re-emerge but they had clearly learnt not to try their luck with us and they were nowhere to be seen. We overturned a couple more cars and then headed to the station to get the train home. We had done them before the game, during the game and after the game. Maybe they would stop and think about the consequences of their actions the next time they considered pulling a blade on someone.

Wigan have got a particularly underhand set of lads. They are always slinking around the place, avoiding our main mob and picking off the stragglers. They are the types who give football hooligans a proper bad name. Whenever you hear on the news about a shirter getting slashed, it's usually mobs like theirs that have carried out the attack. I was glad that we had been able to teach them a lesson and my only regret was that we hadn't managed to do more damage. We should have fucking murdered them for what they did to Big G.

While most mobs will arrange a fight prior to the day of the match, Wigan have a tendency to sneak into their rivals' towns completely unannounced, which has led to people referring to them as the 'Wigan Sneak Squad'. The fact that they believe they are on our level is a fucking joke and they will always be regarded as a group of disreputable wannabes who pick on smaller groups of lads and run for the hills whenever they're faced with our complete firm.

When they aren't moving around in the shadows, hoping that nobody knows they're there, Wigan are usually pulling a complete no show. This has earned them the less-than-favourable nickname of the Invisible Mob to go along with the Sneak Squad name. They were afraid to face us in the 1980s and they're afraid to face us now, as our Great Lever lad can verify . . .

GLL

Wigan don't have the best track record when it comes to turning out for us. In fact they have probably got one of the worst. Even on the rare occasions when they do show up, they will hardly ever stand and fight against a mob with the same numbers. When we played them at home in December 2005 in the League Cup, we ended up spending the entire day looking for them. We might as well have been searching for Bin Laden. We saw nothing of them the whole day, despite the fact that they had been running their mouths off on the internet, saying they were going to do us.

I remember heading off into Bolton on the morning of the match, looking forward to Wigan showing up for a change. We positioned lads at various strategic positions around the town so that they couldn't sneak in unannounced and even spoke to them on the phone to confirm that they were going to turn out. If they didn't show up now they would have no excuse.

Sure enough, we eventually got the word that thirty Wigan lads had landed in Horwich, on the outskirts of the town. We piled into taxis, ready to go and leather them. By the time we got to Horwich, the Old Bill had turned out in force and they were filming us on their cameras, hoping that we would do something illegal so that they could nick us. We ignored them and headed out onto a nearby field, thinking that Wigan might be waiting there to have it with us. We got within a couple of metres of the field when a sixty-strong mob of Bolton lads came charging along the grass. When they got close enough to realise who we were, they stopped dead in their tracks and started laughing. They had obviously thought we were Wigan and we had thought the same about them.

While we were scouring the town, looking for the Goon Squad, the coppers were shutting down the pubs and rounding up our lads. They were determined to prevent a disturbance from taking place and they were stopping and searching people as if it was going out of fashion. It was getting majorly on top so we made our way to the ground, disappointed that Wigan hadn't shown their faces and keeping our fingers crossed that they would be waiting for us after the game.

Nothing of interest happened during the match itself. We lost 2–0, which was a pain in the arse, but Wigan's victory was restricted to the pitch, as they didn't dare to face us. Hundreds of our lads waited for them on the embankment facing the Reebok once the game had finished but we didn't see a single Goon Squad member the whole time we were there. There were a couple of young chavs mouthing off at us from behind the plod but that was the full extent of their resistance.

In a desperate, last-ditch attempt to get a row, we plotted up in the Queen Anne pub on the outskirts of Bolton and waited for our opponents to phone us and tell us where they were. The Old Bill had somehow got wise to us and they were there in no time at all, stopping and searching all and sundry and kicking us out of the boozer before our rivals had a chance to get in touch.

'If you don't fuck off home then you're going to end up getting nicked,' the officer-in-charge threatened.

That was it, our day was over. It was far too on top for us to arrange a fight and none of us fancied a night in the cells so we decided to call it quits. It was a disappointing day for all concerned and we were annoyed at the Invisible Mob for failing to show up. Bolton is only six miles away from Wigan, making Bolton versus Wigan effectively a derby. The fact that they were nowhere to be seen was inexcusable and it confirmed their reputation as the firm that never want to know.

We found out later that Wigan had been hiding behind a set of bushes while we were looking for them in the park. Some of our lads were tooled up to fuck and I have got no doubt in my mind that we would have seriously injured them if we had found them. But what's the point in being a hooligan if you're afraid to have a fight? They wear the clothes and they talk the talk but when it comes to actually having a scrap, they're never within a hundred miles of us. They let themselves down that day and they should hang their heads in shame.

Personally I wouldn't have expected Wigan to turn up in the first place. There have been a couple of occasions when we've had a difficult time finding them and I don't know how they can sneak around the place like that and expect us to take them seriously. If you've gone to somebody's town to kick off then you need to let them know you're there. There is no point standing around and waiting to bump into them by chance. They've got a small handful of decent lads with them but the rest of them might as well not be there.

I remember when we arranged to have a clash with the Goon

Squad at an away game in February 2005. A hundred of our lads met up in Farnworth with the intention of hooking up with the Horwich Casuals, the Tonge Moor Stanley Boys and another mob from Breightmet once we got to Wigan. If we had known how fruitless a journey it was going to be we would have stayed at home. It was another shit day out and it confirmed the fact that Wigan weren't worth our time and effort.

I went to the ground with some of the lads in one of those minibus taxis and the Old Bill followed us the whole way there. Wigan don't need much of an excuse to hide themselves away and an over-the-top amount of coppers on the scene was the last thing that we needed. We parked our vehicle up at Wigan Pier and the minute we opened the doors up ready to step outside, the coppers were all over us like flies on shit. They were fucking everywhere and it was looking increasingly unlikely that we were going to get a row.

As per usual, the Sneak Squad were nowhere to be seen. Lads from Bolton were spread out all across the town so it's not as if we could have missed them. They were doing their standard trick of remaining invisible until we lost interest. After a couple of failed attempts to look for Wigan, we decided to head off to the ground before the Old Bill found an excuse to prevent us from going in. They had already sent a couple of our lads back home to Bolton and we didn't want to be sent home before the match had even started.

We lost 2–1 and despite hearing rumours that Wigan were going to come to the away end after the match, there was still no sign of them. They were keeping well away from us, possibly because there were so many coppers about, but more likely because they didn't want to take us on.

The entire town was flooded with Old Bill and shortly after the game had finished, they herded us into the station and waited at the platform until our train arrived. They even followed us into our carriage to make sure we didn't get back out. There was still a fleeting chance that we were going to get a scrap because word had got round that Wigan's firm would be coming down to Horwich for a last-minute do. As soon as we got back to Bolton, I started desperately sorting minibuses in an attempt to get a mob down there to do them.

I was beginning to think that we would actually get a row when my mate rang and warned me not to bother coming.

'The Old Bill have just turned up,' he told me. 'Everybody's heading home. It's on top as fuck. I'd call it a day if I was you.'

We had tried our hardest to have it with the Goon Squad but it was clearly never going to happen so we reluctantly headed home. We had travelled into their town looking for trouble and walked away without a single punch being thrown. The Old Bill were the best firm on the day by a long shot; they had got everything sussed out from the start. Much as I hate the coppers, at least they turned a mob out for us, which was more than could be said for Wigan.

The Wigan Goon Squad added insult to injury by running their mouths off in Andy Nicholls's book, *Hooligans* (volume two) saying that we only turned out forty-five lads. There were at least two hundred and fifty of us in Wigan that day, not to mention the fifty who were sent back home. What's the point in talking shite in a book when the people that you're talking about are sure to read it? Not only are the Goon Squad never there when you want them to be but they're a bunch of lying fuckers as well. Next time they decide to write about us, they should tell the world how many times we've taken over their town. At least that way it would be believable and we would be able to give them credit for being honest.

29
BURNLEY

There's a direct correlation between how insecure somebody is and how much they feel the need to big themselves up and Andy Porter, 'top boy' of the so-called Burnley Suicide Squad, illustrates this point perfectly. You might remember him from his appearance on Danny Dyer's *The Real Football Factories*, in which he repeatedly proclaimed himself to be the world's hardest man. His autobiography *Suicide Squad: the Inside Story of a Football Firm* was equally self-congratulatory. He seems to chase publicity at every opportunity.

It's funny how Burnley never mentioned Bolton when they were on the telly. Maybe it's got something to do with all the times we've leathered them. I can think of one particular occasion when they were literally begging us to leave them alone. I'll let one of our older lads fill you in on this one.

Older lad

When I think of Burnley, I don't think of their brief stint in the limelight and I definitely don't think of their piece-of-shit book. I think of our home game against them on 1 February 1978, the reason being that I've never seen a mob get that badly leathered in all the time that I've been going to the matches. They got the beating of their lives and it is difficult to see them as the super-firm that Andy Porter makes them out to be after witnessing the frightened looks that were plastered across their faces.

Upon arriving at the stadium that day, I glanced over towards Burnley's end and was distinctly underwhelmed by the amount of lads they had. There were only two hundred there but what they lacked in numbers they made up for in noise. They were hurling abuse in our direction and singing 'Wanky wanky Wanderers', trying to get a rise out of us for the full ninety minutes.

As soon as the game had finished, a couple of hundred Cuckoo Boys headed out of the stadium to lay in wait for Burnley. Most of our lads were tooled up with bricks and bottles and a couple had blades on them. Chanting at us from across the stadium was all well and good but it was time for us to see whether the away fans were capable of handling us on a face-to-face basis.

The Old Bill escorted Burnley out onto Manchester Road, surrounding them with dogs and horses. The coppers were clearly determined to prevent our rivals from getting their heads kicked in but we were intent on getting at them and as they were walking past Orlando Bridge, our entire mob charged along the road towards them. It was time to see what they were made of.

Burnley's firm got fucking annihilated. A skinhead in a yellow jumper got laid flat out with a brick and another of their members was left crying his eyes out, begging a copper for protection. A couple of their boys were on the floor getting kicked to fuck and some of them were even trying to jump on passing buses to get away. So much for them being a mob full of supermen like their book makes them out to be.

Chants of 'Bolton aggro' mingled with the screams of terrified Burnley lads as we laid into them with sticks, bricks and bottles. A couple of them were clinging to the police vans but there was no escaping from us. I have never seen a group of so-called hooligans look as terrified as them. Some of them were paralysed with fear.

Burnley were supposedly nicknamed the Suicide Squad a couple of years down the line because they were always willing to battle against the odds. Well that's a crock of shite if ever I heard one. They didn't stand and fight against us; they cried their fucking eyes out. Andy Porter, if you're reading this, the next time you write a book I want you to include a chapter on all the times we've done you. It would at least qualify your book for the non-fiction section, as opposed to fantasy.

Andy Porter and his hunger for fame aside, we have had some decent rows with the Suicide Squad. They have never been the best of firms but we had a fearsome run-in with them in the Eighties, known as the Battle of Turf Moor. Here's Phil to fill you in on what went down.

Phil

It was a foggy Tuesday night and Bolton had taken a huge following to Burnley. Something always went off whenever we played them so we knew that they'd be up for it. Sure enough, towards the end of the game, lads from both teams started taking up their positions, ready for it to go. The final whistle went and Burnley swarmed onto the pitch, egging the Bolton fans on to bring it. And bring it we did.

Within the space of a split second, there were scuffles going on all over the pitch and mounted police were charging about the place, trying to put a stop to the action. They eventually managed to herd us back into our ends but some Burnley lads managed to get in with us, resulting in running battles all around the terracing.

The Old Bill steamed in and interrupted the brawls but, by that stage, it was already too late. We had damaged the ground and we had damaged one another. Both mobs had been intent on winning the fight and the coppers were powerless to bring the violence to a halt until we had done what we set out to do. It was another epic battle and one that our lads still talk about today. The Battle of Turf Moor, what a fucking night!

Second hand copies of *Suicide Squad: the Inside Story of a Football Firm* are selling for 1p each on Amazon and that's no word of a lie. Fair enough, Burnley's mob have got their good points but Andy Porter hasn't done them any favours. Their lads may have provided us with a couple of decent battles, such as the one that Phil has just described, but that's no reason for them to go on like they're superhuman. The truth will always come out in the end, regardless of what some clueless idiot decides to write in a book.

30
LEST WE FORGET . . .

Here is a quick summary of some of the games that I've not had chance to cover elsewhere in the book. I wouldn't want to miss anything out.

Southend away, 27 August 1988
We had a big piss up during the match. Some of the lads sprawled out on the terraces and fell asleep. At half-time, loads of our lads ran onto the pitch and across to Southend's end. Southend ran on after us but ended up getting slapped. The Old Bill put a stop to the action by coming out with their dogs.

Port Vale away, 15 October 1988
They attempted to take our pub before the game and one of them ended up with stab wounds to his throat and wrist, a severed ear and two missing fingers. He needed over forty stitches.

The Vale lads got the upper hand and legged the Bolton mob into B&Q but our lot quickly tooled themselves up from the shelves and turned the situation round. Some of us armed ourselves with Stanley knives and screwdrivers and one mad cunt picked up a spade. Now that we were better equipped, we went back outside and stood our ground.

The violence eventually came to a halt and we headed into the stadium to watch the game. Towards the end of the match, our entire mob went charging across the terraces and attempted to get over the concrete wall that separated us from them. Nobody can accuse us of waiting for them to come to us.

Fleetwood away, 2 August 1986

We took a good two hundred and fifty lads with us, which isn't bad for a pre-season friendly. A few of us climbed over the stadium wall and got in without paying.

We had a brief confrontation with some Blackpool lads during the second half. Once we had finished having it with them, word got round that they had a mob out for us in Memorial Park so we climbed back over the wall to see if they were there. Blackpool had teamed up with some lads from a nearby fair and we had a second round with them. The two sides pelted one another with bottles and stones and the coppers had to bring in canine units to get the situation under control.

York City away, 2 March 1987

There were three matches left and we had to win at least two of them or we would be relegated to division four. We lost 2–1, which didn't exactly make for a peaceful game.

It went off in the York stand and we ended up rowing with the fans in the stand to our left. One of our lot got nicked and as the arresting officer was slapping on the cuffs, the copper's helmet fell off and somebody set about him with it. He didn't half get a hiding and it was funny as fuck to see him getting leathered with his own hat. After the match had finished, one of our younger lads jumped in the river Ouse for a bet. The crazy cunt!

Bradford City at home, 6 May 1985

Bradford were top of the table and we knew there would be thousands of them in attendance. There was trouble in the town centre for a good three hours before kickoff and it went off like fuck in the Burnden Paddock during the game. Lumps of concrete and hefty wooden seats went flying about the place and a copper got hit on the head with a brick, fracturing his skull.

Swindon at home, 23 August 1986

It was the first game of the season and the atmosphere inside the ground was tense as fuck. Coins were whistling through the air and one of our supporters got hit and lost an eye.

We twatted Swindon's firm with lumps of concrete and wood after the game had finished. A carload of their lads mounted the kerb in their hurry to get away. They were lucky that they were in their car or we would have fucking leathered them.

Leeds United at home, 30 November 1977

The police did everything that they could to prevent it from going off once the game had finished. They pushed our fans up the Manny Road towards Bolton town centre and kept the Leeds supporters in the Embankment End. Canine units and mounted police patrolled the streets, ready to pounce on anyone who stepped out of line.

We were determined to have it, Old Bill or no Old Bill, and as the Leeds Service Crew were being escorted to the station lads jumped out of their cars to get at them. The police charged in on their horses, herding us up Bradshawgate, where the road had been closed off. A group of Bolton lads managed to break away from the main mob and they stormed into our rivals at the bottom of Trinity Street. The coppers pushed them back and hurried the Leeds fans into the station before anything else flared off.

West Ham at home, 28 March 1981

There were a few minor scuffles in Bolton town centre before the game started but nothing to write home about. The first proper kickoff happened during the second half in the Manny Road South End. It was proper toe to toe and there must have been a good hundred and fifty lads involved. I was in the paddock opposite, watching everybody going mental.

At the end where it was going off the coppers pushed and shoved at the gate but they couldn't get it open. When they finally managed to get to where the action was, all you could see was police helmets flying about in the air as they struggled to regain order. It was ages before they managed to stop the brawl. Fair play to West Ham, they came for it and they got it.

Chesterfield away, 28 February 1987

There was trouble all across the town before the game and quite a few arrests. The action continued inside the ground, with skirmishes taking place in the corner near the floodlights, next to the Chesterfield end. We went toe to toe with Chesterfield's mob until the Old Bill let their dogs loose. A couple of lads got bit and others tried to climb the fencing to get away.

It went off again outside the stadium after the final whistle had blown. There were running battles up and down the streets and a few more arrests were made.

Scarborough away, 29 August 1987

I have been told there were a few scuffles in the town centre prior to the game but I didn't see anything go off until we got inside the stadium. During the second half, the Scarborough fans started lobbing coins at us so we charged towards the fencing to get at them. Some of our lads climbed over the fence and a brawl ensued. Riot police were eventually drafted in to put an end to the disturbances.

After the game, we were confined to our end and the Scarborough lads were kept on the edge of the pitch to prevent us from going at it. A line of dog-handlers separated the two mobs. When they finally let us out, someone threw a bottle of cider at one of the police horses and smacked it full in the face. Lads went weaving in and out of the traffic, looking for a fight, and a group of barmy cunts lay down in the middle of the road to stop the cars from moving. It was a chaotic ending to a chaotic day.

Arsenal at home, 16 February 1980

We didn't have to wait too long for it to kick off, as there was a brawl in the car park outside Burnden Park before the game. One of our lads got whacked from behind and a copper grabbed him by his hair and dragged him along the floor to the Lever End.

When we got inside the ground, one of our lot ran into a group of twenty Arsenal lads in the Burnden Paddock. He started setting about them with a crate of milk and the rest of our mob steamed in after him. The Arsenal boys got a bit of a kicking and had to jump the fence onto the pitch to get away.

Arsenal were determined to even up the score. Two hundred of their lads ran round to the Burnden Paddock as some of our lads left the ground and legged them onto the banking opposite the stadium. The Old Bill were intent on baton-charging people about the place but that wasn't going to stop us getting back at our opponents. We charged straight through a line of coppers and into a group of Gooners, sparking off a series of running battles right along Manny Road.

We eventually got the upper hand and backed Arsenal's mob off into the station. They were game as fuck and they had a good two hundred lads out. I know one of their lads through the EDL and I've since been told they had already had a run-in with a group of Mancs prior to meeting us. We were their second brawl of the day, which shows how up-for-it they were.

Barnsley away, 9 January 1988

It went off majorly in the away end, mostly with the Old Bill. The action carried on outside and ended in a three-way brawl between Bolton, Barnsley and the police.

In the wake of the disturbances, Richard Gray of the South Yorkshire police force stated that groups of Bolton fans had been circling the town centre, in search of home fans to attack. He stressed that the trouble was caused by a 'mindless minority', which is the usual response from the coppers.

'A lot of idiots follow football these days but Bolton seem to have more than most,' a police spokesman told the *Bolton Evening News*. 'They are worse than the notorious Birmingham, Leeds and Chelsea fans.'

Rotherham away, 18 January 1986

We invaded the home end during the game and had it with the Old Bill after it had finished. One of our lads had a bit of a wrestling match with a police dog and would have come out on top if the coppers hadn't nicked him.

Darlington away, 1 May 1986

There was trouble all game long and, after the match had finished, the action spilled onto the pitch. The locals were all proper up for it and a couple of people got stabbed. Darlington is one hell of a tough town.

Southampton at home, 27 April 1996

It was the last game of the season and we were as good as relegated. When Southampton scored, their fans started climbing the fencing at the corner of the Burnden Paddock. We jumped on the fence to get at them and they backed off.

As the game came to an end, a load of our lads started shaking the fencing, trying to get into the away end. Some pieces of concrete crumbled away from the bottom of the divide and we levelled them at the Southampton fans. The police attempted to intervene and one of them got hit in the face with a rock.

Not content with pelting our rivals with stones, we left the stadium and headed up the steps at the back of the away end. Southampton ran like fuck onto their coaches. The Old Bill were the only ones that had the balls to face us, although they had their four-legged friends to help them. One of my mates got a huge chunk bitten off the back of his leg by a dog and I was bitten on the arm as I came to his aid. It was a shit day all round. Southampton were mouthy but not at all up for it and those police dogs were mad.

Queens Park Rangers at home, 5 April 1997

QPR didn't bring many lads with them. Most of their support consisted of shirters and families and there were a lot of kids there. Steve Morrow scored a cracking goal for QPR and a handful of Bolton lads kicked it off in their end. Some of the QPR mob ran at them but they stood their ground and fought. There were only half a dozen of our lot there and we were badly outnumbered. The brave Boltonians ended up backing off and scuffling their way up the terraces to the exit.

31
BOLTON VERSUS BOLTON

Bolton's mob has always been made up of a series of smaller, independent firms and although the majority of them tend to get on well, we have been plagued by internal conflicts in recent years. Infighting causes serious complications and it isn't good for anyone but despite the negative effect that it has had on our mob, there are certain bitter rivalries that are unlikely to be resolved any time soon.

By far the most serious of our internal feuds is that between the Tonge Moor Stanley Boys and the Great Lever mob. Lads from the two areas can't even drink in the same pubs without it going off. This has caused a massive rift in our firm and split us up in two. I couldn't even begin to tell you what the original reason for the conflict was, although it is rumoured to have escalated from an argument at a game against Cardiff in which a lad's drink was spilt. It is a shame because, at the end of the day, we all support Bolton and we should be pooling our efforts to fight with rival teams, rather than squabbling among ourselves. The sooner we agree to put our differences aside and come together as one, the stronger we will be.

Although the Tonge Moor versus Great Lever rivalry is the most intense dispute within the mob, there are a number of different areas in the town that are at odds. Tonge Moor and Halliwell have fallen out with Astley Bridge in recent years, there have been confrontations between Deane and Breightmet and the Farnworth lot have had numerous run-ins with groups of lads from Bolton. Most of these feuds have escalated from minor incidents, although several have led to major altercations. The battle that Little Lever had with Tonge Moor back in 1995 was one such occasion. Little Lever resident Phil can fill you in on exactly what went down . . .

Phil

It was 9 December 1995 and word had got about that fifteen Tonge Moor lads had been involved in a scuffle with at a couple of lads from Little Lever. If it was even numbers then we wouldn't have got involved but they had been taking liberties with our mates so we headed off into town to see if they were about.

Tonge Moor is basically just your average working-class area but there are a lot of football lads round there and they always turn out in numbers. Both mobs ended up going to a club called 5th Avenue in Bolton town centre and one of their boys came over to our lot, giving it the biggie and running his mouth off to my friend's brother.

'Don't let a knobhead like that talk to your brother like that,' I told my mate, 'Just get into him.'

For whatever reason, none of the other lads were doing anything so I pushed my way to the front of our mob and gave the mouthy fucker a smack. This seemed to spur the rest of the Little Lever lot into action and one of them picked up a heavy wooden barstool and flung it at the Tonge Moor contingent. Within minutes, glasses and bottles were flying about the place and a full-scale bar brawl was going off.

Both of our mobs ended up in a pretty nasty state. I got sliced across my fingers with a Stanley blade and needed six stitches, although I didn't even realise what had happened to me until I went to hospital to get myself checked out. 'It's definitely a knife wound,' the nurse informed me, although I'm still not entirely sure that it was. There was so much broken glass flying about that I could have cut myself in any number of different ways.

For a lot of people in Bolton, their knife is like their car keys; they never leave the house without it. You can say what you want about blades but they're a naughty thing to have on you and nothing strikes fear into the heart of an opponent like a Stanley knife. The Tonge Moor lot were famous for carrying tools and they had sliced, cut, hacked and slashed their fair share of rivals down the years. If they had in fact used a blade on me then I was just another victim to add to their collection.

We were playing Liverpool at home the day after the disturbance and shortly after I arrived at the ground, I was approached by a couple of neutral faces, who tipped me off that a big group of Tonge Moor lads were looking for lads from Little Lever.

'It's best to keep a low profile,' they warned. 'They're out for revenge.'

I was on my own at the time so I decided to take their advice. I gave the game a miss and headed off to my local boozer instead. To be honest it was a fairly typical occurrence. Every time there was a fight, a group of lads from one of the warring areas would go out looking for their rivals a couple of days later and the conflict would go on and on. Some of the mobs that were feuding back then are still at odds with one another to this very day and there doesn't seem to be an end in sight. Bolton has always been territorial and there have always been turf wars. It is part and parcel of life round here and it is what you come to expect.

It is a sad state of affairs when you think we could be pulling mobs of up to five hundred lads together but internal disputes are preventing that from happening. Perhaps Phil is right and the division that exists in the firm stems from the cliquey attitude of people from our town. None of the areas in Bolton and Farnworth have ever mixed particularly well and it's holding us back in a major way. Maybe one day we will put our differences aside and attack our enemies as one but, until that day occurs, a lot of time and effort will be wasted squabbling amongst ourselves.

32

OPERATION GAMMA

Although the infighting between the different Bolton firms contributed significantly to our downfall, it was nothing compared to the events of May 1990, when the coppers took steps to eradicate us once and for all. There had been a number of high-profile acts of hooliganism in the news and the Bolton Old Bill were being put under increasing amounts of pressure to take us off the streets. Operation Gamma was their attempt to wipe us out. It was the biggest-ever crackdown on hooligan gangs and it indicated a marked change in the police's attitude towards football violence. Gone were the days when they would give you a clip around the ear hole and send you on your way. Thanks to the tabloid press, firms like ours were now seen as public enemy number one and the coppers were willing to spend vast amounts of money to have us put away.

The operation hinged around six Old Bill from the Merseyside Constabulary infiltrating our mob and providing evidence against us. We have always had lads from a number of different towns with us, which leaves us open to undercovers, as it makes our membership difficult to keep track of. We've had lads from Wigan, Blackpool, Chorley, Rochdale, Manchester, Salford and even Airdrie in our firm over the years so we didn't see it as anything out of the ordinary when a group of Scousers suddenly started coming to the matches with us. The Old Bill had only just started major operations against football hooligans and we were still relatively naïve about the whole process. We are a lot more wary nowadays and I am certain it will never happen again.

Looking back, it isn't hard to tell who the undercovers were. One of them got nicked at a game against Blackpool and the coppers let him go. That should have immediately aroused our suspicion but, over time, they gathered enough evidence to convict thirty-four of our lads, with the harshest punishment handed out being a three-year custodial sentence. S was one of the lads who got arrested. He was living at his mum's house on the day of the raids and she wasn't best pleased. Here's his account of what went on . . .

S

'What have you done now?' my old lady screamed. 'I knew this would happen if you carried on going to the football.'

Two plain-clothes officers and two uniformed coppers came striding into the house to search for evidence and panic quickly set in.

'Mr S, I am arresting you for your involvement in organized football violence throughout the country during the period of 1988–1989,' the arresting officer told me. 'You do not have to say anything but anything that you do say may be used in evidence against you in a court of law.'

Another copper slapped on a pair of handcuffs and escorted me to my room, where his colleagues conducted a thorough search of my belongings. They uncovered two smoke bombs and several items of clothing that I had worn to the games, which provided them with more than enough rope to hang me with.

Over the next two days, I was interviewed about my activities at various matches, including Sheffield United away on 4 February 1989, Port Vale away on 15 October 1988, Blackpool away on 18 February 1989 and Wolves away on 3 March 1989. I was also questioned about disturbances at a number of rugby-league games that had taken place at Burnden Park during the course of 1988 and 1989, including Leeds versus Wigan, Wigan versus Swinton and Salford versus Wigan. We had started turning out for Wigan rugby to give us something to do when there wasn't any football. The coppers must have got wind of it and decided to come along. Now they would be able to brand me as one of Britain's first convicted rugby hooligans!

I was eventually granted bail on the condition that I had to report to the local police station every time there was a match on. As far as I was concerned, it was all a fuss about nothing. I had been defending my town from invaders.

What was so bad about that? It wasn't as if I was out attacking innocent members of the public. Still, the sooner I could get it over and done with, the sooner I could return to normality.

During the court case, the prosecution described how 'ringleaders' commanded armies of up to three hundred people, ordering them to smash up the pubs that rival hooligans were drinking in. They claimed that some of our members were involved in Protestant extremism and also that Nazi salutes had been made at our games.

'There has been a positive campaign of vilification orchestrated, it would appear, by the police at some level,' defence barrister James Gregory argued. 'It is wholly improper.'

He pointed out that none of the undercover officers had seen any of us using weapons and he attempted to make out that we were overzealous football fans as opposed to fully fledged hooligans. At least somebody was there to fight our corner.

I was originally charged with eight separate offences, although my solicitor managed to get four of them dropped in return for a guilty plea. I confessed to four counts of conspiracy to cause affray and my sentencing date was set for 18 May, giving me another month of worry before hearing my fate.

While I was anxiously waiting to hear how long I was going to get, the press were having a fucking field day. 'Wanderers' wreckers must pay the price', read the headline of a special report published in the Bolton Evening News. 'A court has heard how Bolton hooligans exported violence nationwide. ... The thugs, who waged war with smoke-bombs, fought inside and outside football grounds and pubs. They even tried to pick fights with Rugby League fans.'

Once again, football hooligans were being made out to be the scum of the earth by the papers, although we had more important things to worry about than a bunch of third-rate hacks slagging us off. Our day of reckoning was rapidly drawing closer and we were about to find out how long we were going to get.

On the day we were due to be sentenced, we arrived at Liverpool Crown Court full of dread. I met some of my co-defendants at the entrance to the building and we started discussing what the likely outcome was going to be.

'Do you think it will all have been worth it if you end up going to jail?' one of the other lads asked me.

'Yeah,' I replied. 'We were only defending our town.'

As it happened, we might as well have stayed at home, because the judge announced that we had to wait until the twenty-first to pass sentence. However, rather than allowing us to spend our last few days of freedom saying goodbye to our families, he refused to renew our bail and we were taken to HMP Walton in Liverpool, where we were to remain until he came to a decision.

'Nine Bolton thugs spent last night in custody awaiting their fate in Britain's biggest ever soccer hooligan trial,' journalist Paul Breakwell wrote in the Bolton Evening News. '*Judge Donald Hart decided not to renew their bail as a warning to make sure all charged fans are at Liverpool Crown Court when he starts sentencing for a series of offences relating to hooliganism and race-hate thuggery. The judge has ordered the forfeiture of knives, a knuckle-duster and four pointed finger dusters seized from their homes. He will be asked to order them to forfeit other items seized, including hooligan "calling cards" and a wooden stick with a nail in the end.*'

By the time my sentencing date arrived, I was prepared for the worst. I took my seat in the dock and the judge immediately started ripping into me, calling me every name under the sun.

'You are a disgrace to mankind and a disgrace to the general public,' he told me. 'Football would be a lot better off without people like you. I thereby sentence you to serve a two-year custodial sentence.'

Two years was fairly lenient, all things considered. I had already been given two separate banning orders for previous offences and I could have been given a lot longer. As I was led away to the holding cells underneath the court, I remember reflecting upon the mayhem I had caused following my beloved Bolton Wanderers over the years and thinking that I was lucky to have got away so lightly. At least it was all over and done with and there was nothing left hanging over me.

I started my sentence off in HMP Walton and I was transferred to HMP Haverigg in the Lake District part way through my stint. Haverigg was like a holiday camp. I was allowed to go home to see my family at Christmas and if I didn't have any visitors on a Sunday the prison authorities would let me out to go on hiking trips in the nearby countryside. When I wasn't hiking or at home, I spent my time playing football for the prison team and working in the aviaries at Munster castle in Ravenglass. Prison was a walk in the park and the months flew by.

On the day of my release, I left prison feeling sad that I had to leave the friends I had made behind. My family were crying tears of joy that I had finally been allowed to go free but I couldn't help thinking that I was going to miss the good times inside. Still, it was all behind me now and I was going back to Bolton to continue where I had left off.

Operation Gamma wasn't the last time I was in trouble with the law. Since then I have been arrested twice: against Birmingham at home and at an away game against Tranmere, although I was lucky enough to get a caution on both occasions. Nowadays I've got a decent job and a beautiful seven-year-old daughter so I'm very much retired from the scene. Hooliganism was good while it lasted but there are more important things in life than fighting at the matches. Saying that though, my memories will stay with me forever and I've got stories coming out of my ears. I may not be an active hooligan anymore but I have stayed in touch with what's going on and I will always be a football lad at heart.

Operation Gamma paved the way for expensive, time-consuming police initiatives, aimed at putting hooligans behind bars. It was the first time that the Old Bill had spent such a large amount of money on going after us and the fact that it secured so many successful convictions cemented its effectiveness in the minds of the authorities. It blazed a trail for similar operations in the years to come.

Nowadays you have to be a lot more careful about who you allow into the inner circle, as undercovers are a standard hazard faced by hooligans up and down the country. The coppers are waging a bitter war against us but no matter what they do football violence will always be an integral part of the game. It is part and parcel of working-class culture in Britain and it will never go away. The Bolton Old Bill can try their hardest to lock us up but we will always find a way of counteracting whatever methods they use against us. As long as there are lads who enjoy a good punch up, the Cuckoo Boys will carry on their reign of terror undaunted.

33
THE FUTURE

Although we are still going strong in spite of Operation Gamma and our various internal conflicts, football hooliganism isn't what it used to be. During the 1970s, we were having regular mass brawls with up to a thousand people on either side, whereas nowadays it is rare when mobs with a couple of hundred lads apiece turn out. Advances in technology have put a stop to the days of huge, spontaneous riots. CCTV has sprung up everywhere and face-recognition software has made banning orders easier for the coppers to enforce. Don't get me wrong, you still get some naughty little fights involving twenty to thirty lads but it's really not the same. The 1970s and the 1980s were the golden era of football violence and nothing can ever come close to the levels of excitement that we experienced in those halcyon days. It was an exhilarating time to be alive and I would do it all again, given half the chance.

The increase in CCTV installations and banning orders has, of necessity, led to better planning and organisation. Although violence inside stadiums has become a lot rarer, the current generation of hooligans have taken to arranging their fights in out-of-the-way places where the coppers are less likely to get onto them. Whereas the streets around the stadiums are now relatively trouble free, more obscure locations where we don't have to worry about being caught on camera are being transformed into battlegrounds.

Mobile phones mean that rival firms can get in contact with each other prior to the matches to discuss where they want to go at it. The

Old Bill have undercover spotters at the games so the grounds are no longer a viable place for us to go to work on our opponents. The 'football' part of 'football hooliganism' is gradually taking a backseat and the violence is not necessarily an accompaniment to a sporting event. More often than not, our younger lads will travel into a rival firm's town to have a do even when there isn't a match on, proving that our hooligans will always adapt to whatever preventative measures the coppers put in place.

A lot of the younger generation will kick off in full view of the CCTV if there is no other option available. Growing up in a Big Brother society has given them a thicker skin about things like that and a lot of them really don't seem to give a fuck if they get arrested or not. They are a lot less wary than we were at their age and most of them are banned already.

In addition to the advances in policing, the emergence of rave culture also had a major negative effect on the football-violence scene. During the early Nineties, drugs like ecstasy and LSD were rapidly gaining in popularity and you had former rivals mixing at acid-house events, loved up on Es and chatting away to one another like the best of mates. A fair few of them were into supplying drugs as well, which meant they had to get on with lads from other firms in order to make money from them.

When you have been hugging someone and dancing about in an ecstasy-fuelled stupor, I imagine it is pretty difficult to get stuck into them a couple of days later, which meant that the intensity of match-day violence declined. You had the likes of Millwall and West Ham attending the same events without so much as a single punch being thrown, which would never have happened if it wasn't for drugs. And then there was the harder stuff. Some of the lads got involved in heroin and a couple of them got completely hooked. I stayed well away from that scene, which turned out to be a very wise move when I consider the number who died because of drugs, not to mention those who got addicted.

Although I still see a lot of the other Bolton lads at EDL events, I am now officially retired from the world of football violence. When I was younger, I didn't give a fuck and I would fight with anybody for any reason. But I met my wife Dianne twenty-nine years ago, in 1982, and I began to settle down. From 1984 to 1988 I only went to certain games, as money was tight and I was in and out of work with two kids and a young wife to look after. After that I got right back into it in a big way but then, four years ago, Dianne was diagnosed with cancer. That was when I really started to move away from the hooligan scene and instead focused on my family. Nowadays I prefer to go to the grounds purely to watch the games. The violence was fun while it lasted but there comes a time when every football lad has to hang up his gloves. I quit while I was ahead.

I have some cracking memories and I will never forget the friends I made through supporting Bolton. Nowadays, however, I have no desire to go to the matches looking for a fight. This book is my way of shutting the lid on that chapter of my life once and for all. To all the lads who have fought side by side with me over the years, I wish you all the best and I would like to thank you for the exciting times we had together. We stuck together through thick and thin and none of this would have been possible without you. S, Graham, Chris, Phil and everybody else who has gone to the games with us, this means you.

THE LINGO

In an effort to remain true to the way that we talk, throughout the course of this book I have used dialect, slang and jargon that the average person may not be familiar with. Here is a quick rundown of anything that might be likely to cause confusion.

Baggies	West Brom fans
Beer monster	an older hooligan, usually with a beer belly
Bin-dipper	Scouser
Brief	a solicitor
Boozer	a pub
Boy	a younger hooligan with a distinctive style of dress
Casual	somebody who dresses in terrace fashions
Ching	cocaine
Chinged up	on cocaine
Dibble/OB/Old Bill/plod	police
Done	beaten
Dresser	an early form of casual
Faces	well-known hooligans
Firm/mob	a gang
Game	up for a fight
Gooners	Arsenal fans
Invisible Mob/Sneak Squad	nicknames given to the Wigan Goon

	Squad, taking the piss out of them for sneaking into other people's towns completely unannounced
Jib	avoid paying in to somewhere
Lad	a hooligan
Munich	a Man United supporter
On your toes	running away
Pot	a glass
Potted	hit with a glass
Seasiders	Blackpool fans
Section 60	stop and search
Shirter/shirt-wearer/scarfer	a football fan who isn't a hooligan
Snide	counterfeit
Stand	stay and fight
Sweaty Sock	Jock
Taking liberties	taking the Mickey
Weighed in	beaten up
Whiz	amphetamine